ALSO BY FENTON JOHNSON

Scissors, Paper, Rock

Crossing the River

Larry Rose
Brasserie Terminus Nord
PARIS 1988

GEOGRAPHY

OF THE

HEART

A Memoir

FENTON JOHNSON

SCRIBNER

SCRIBNER
1230 Avenue of the Americas
New York, NY 10020

SCRIBNER and design are
trademarks of Simon & Schuster Inc.

Set in Adobe Perpetua
Designed by Jennifer Daddio

Manufactured in the United States of America

1   3   5   7   9   10   8   6   4   2

Library of Congress Cataloging-in-Publication Data
Johnson, Fenton.
Geography of the heart : a memoir / Fenton Johnson.
p.   cm.
1. Rose, Larry 1949–1990. 2. Johnson, Fenton.
3. Gay men—United States—Biography.
4. HIV infections—Patients—United States—Biography.
5. Gay male couples—United States—Biography.
6. Bereavement—United States. I. Title.
HQ75.8R67J65   1996
305.38'9664'0922—dc20   95-53070
CIP
ISBN 0-684-81417-X

See page 239 for text permissions.

. . . of course

loss is the great lesson.

MARY OLIVER, "Poppies"

DEDICATION

In the months following Larry's death, this is what I set out to do: To present some sense of what it meant for two people to be in love in a particular place in time, because I believed that if I could present such a story cleanly and plainly enough it would have the power to move hearts (so much more fixed than mountains). Now, at the end of this particular journey, I can say that it provided me a way back, a means of coming home.

I dedicate my labor on this book to those who gave and continue to give their time and lives to preventing the spread of HIV/AIDS; to those who have helped and are helping persons with the disease; to those who are ill; to those who have died. I thank especially the men and women who in necessary and appropriate exercise of their right to free speech interrupted the remarks of U.S. Health and Human Services secretary Louis Sullivan to the International AIDS Conference in San Francisco in June 1990.

Reading is the unsurpassed interactive act, and serious readers among the least acknowledged and appreciated of revolutionaries. This book is for Larry, who read, and you, who are reading.

Acknowledgments and Thanks

Portions of this book have appeared in different form in *Mother Jones* magazine, *The New York Times Magazine, San Francisco Focus*, and in the anthologies *How We Live Now* and *In the Company of My Solitude*.

The following are among the many friends and colleagues who contributed to or significantly shaped my thinking about this work. Much of what is good originated with them; the faults I claim as my own. For their comments, suggestions, advice, and ideas, I am deeply grateful to Peter Adair, Caroline Colburn Armstrong, Haney Armstrong, Malaga Baldi, Susan Brenneman, Jane Clayton, Douglas Foster, Bill Grose, Rich Hendry, Barry Owen, Jane Rosenman, Jay Schaefer, Louis Schump, and Katherine Seligman. Thanks also to the Headlands Center for the Arts for its support and working space.

I reserve my deepest gratitude for the members of our families, Larry's and mine, who have so generously entrusted me with their stories, and whose love and support enabled us to love each other and ourselves. I single out for special thanks Larry's parents, Fred and Kathy Rose.

From respect for their privacy, I have changed the names of some of the people of our lives.

GEOGRAPHY OF THE HEART

PROLOGUE/POSTSCRIPT

It is late March—the Saturday of Passover, 1991, to be exact—and I am driving an oversize rented car through west Los Angeles. This side of the city I have never seen except in the company of my lover Larry Rose, who died of AIDS in a Paris hospital some six months earlier.

He was an only child, who asked more than once that I promise to visit his parents after his death. Youngest son of a large family and a believer in brutal honesty, I'd refused. I have too much family already, I told him. There are limits to how much love I can give.

Now I am driving along one of the lovelier streets of Santa Monica, San Vicente Boulevard, west from Wilshire to the Pacific. The street is divided by a broad green median lined with coral trees, which the city has seen fit to register as landmarks. They spread airy, elegant crowns against a movie-set heaven, a Maxfield Parrish blue. Each branch bleeds at its tip an impossibly scarlet blossom, as if the limbs themselves had pierced the thin-skinned sky.

Larry's parents, Fred and Kathy Rose, are too old to get about much. They are German Jews, who spent the war years hiding in a Dutch village a few miles from Germany itself. Beaten by Nazis before the war, Fred hid for three years with broken vertebrae, unable to see a doctor. When he was no longer able to move, Kathy descended to the street to find help, to see falling from the sky the parachutes of their liberators. After the war they married and came to California, promised land of this promised land. Like Abraham and Sarah, in their advanced years they had a single son; proof that it is possible, in the face of the worst, to pick up sticks and start again.

Fred greets me at the door of their small bungalow. Even in mourning he wears his customary suit and tie, but he seems smaller than in my earlier visits. In his bent and shrunken frame I understand how Larry was a shield against his memories, and now Larry is gone.

Fred, Kathy, and I sit to talk, but Fred is reserved; he does not talk about Larry with the women of his life—his wife or his surviving sister. No doubt he fears giving way before his grief, and his life has not allowed for much giving way. This much he and I share: a gay man who grew up in the rural South, I am no stranger to hiding.

Kathy always goes to bed early—partly by way of coping with grief—but this evening Fred all but asks her to retire. After she leaves, he begins talking of Larry, and I listen and respond with gratefulness. We are two men in control, who permit ourselves to speak to each other of our loss because we subscribe implicitly, jointly, unconditionally to this code of conduct.

Fred tells a familiar story, of the day when Larry, then eight years old, wanted to go fishing. The quintessential urban Jew, Fred nonetheless bought poles and hooks and drove fifty miles to Laguna Beach. There they dropped their lines from a pier to discover the hooks dangled some ten feet above the water. "Thank God," Fred says. "Otherwise we might have caught something." A passerby scoffed, "What the hell do you think you're trying to catch?" Fred shrugged, unperturbed. "Flying fish," he said.

I respond with my most vivid memory of my time with Larry. A wiser man than I, he spoke many times of his great luck, his great good fortune. "I'm so lucky," he said again and again. Denial pure and simple, or so I told myself in our first years together. AZT, ddI, ACT-UP, CMV, DHPG, and what I came to think of as the big "A" itself—he endured this acronymed life, while I listened and participated and helped when I could.

Until our third and final trip to Paris, when on our last night to walk about the city, we sat in the courtyard of the Picasso Museum. There under a dusk-deep sky I turned to him and said, "I'm so lucky," and it was as if the time allotted to him to teach me this lesson, the time allotted to me to learn it, had been consumed, and there was nothing left but the facts of things to play out.

A long pause after this story—I have ventured beyond what I permit myself, what I am permitted.

I change the subject, asking Fred to talk of the war years. He speaks not of his beating or of murdered family and friends but of moments of affection, loyalty, even humor, until he speaks of winters spent confined to bed, huddled in Kathy's arms, their breaths freezing on the quilt as they sang together to pass time, to stay warm, to distract him from his pain, to ward off their fear.

Another silence. Now he has ventured too far. "I have tried to forget these stories," he says in his halting English.

In the presence of these extremes of love and sorrow I am reduced to cliché. "It's only by remembering them that we can hope to avoid repeating them," I say.

"They are being repeated all the time," Fred says. "It is bad sometimes to watch too much television. You see these things and you know we have learned nothing."

Are we so dense that we can learn nothing from all this pain, all this death? Is it impossible to learn from experience? The bitterness of these questions I can taste, as I drive east to spend the night at a relative's apartment.

Just south of the seedier section of Santa Monica Boulevard I stop at a bar recommended by a friend. I need a drink, I need the company of men like myself—survivors, for the moment anyway, albeit of a very different struggle.

The bar is filled with Latino drag queens wearing extraordinary clothes. Eighty years of B movies have left Hollywood the nation's most remarkable supply of secondhand dresses, many of which, judging from this evening, have made their ways to these men's closets.

I am standing at the bar, very Anglo, very out of place, very much thinking of leaving, when a tiny, wizened, gray-haired Latina approaches the stage, where under jerry-built lights (colored cello-phane, Scotch tape) a man lip-synchs to Brazilian rock. His spike heels raise him to something more than six feet; he wears a floor-length sheath dress slit up the sides and so taut, so brilliantly silver, so lustrous that it catches and throws back the faces of his audience. The elderly Latina raises a dollar bill. On tottering heels he lowers himself, missing not a word of his song while half-crouching, half-bending so that she may tuck her dollar in his cleavage and kiss his cheek.

"*Su abuelita,*" the bartender says. "His grandmother."

One A.M. in the City of Angels—the streets are clogged with cars. Stuck in traffic, I am haunted by voices and visions: by the high, thin songs of Fred and Kathy as they huddle under their frozen quilt, singing into their breaths; by a small boy and his father sitting on a very long pier, their baitless fishhooks dangling above the vast Pacific; by the face of *su abuelita,* uplifted and ador-ing, mirrored in her grandson's dress.

Somewhere a light changes; the traffic unglues itself. As cars begin moving, I am visited by two last ghosts—myself and Larry Rose, sitting in the courtyard of the Hôtel Salé, transfigured by the limitless heart.

My life with Larry Rose came to this: The two of us driving down a country road in France, a river's silver mirror showing now broad and shining, now slivered into shards by limbs and leaves of yellowing willows and lindens. The autumn light fading too fast from the sky. The two of us consumed with love, and his dying.

I knew Larry slightly more than three years—we met in late summer 1987; he died October 17, 1990. Anyone who's had the good fortune to love and be loved for ten or twenty or forty and more years may doubt the significance of such a short time, and in light of those years I understand.

But love doesn't measure itself by the calendar (does a mother love her child less because he is young?). It's possible to live a lifetime of love in three years—for so many people in these times, not only possible but necessary. What follows are stories from those years: how he, a teacher, taught me how to love; how slowly I learned what he had to teach.

Emigrant Sons

Engraved on the interior walls of the monument honoring those deported during the Nazi occupation of France:

J'ai rêvé tellement fort de toi—j'ai tellement marché, tellement parlé, tellement aimé ton ombre qu'il ne me reste plus rien de toi—il me reste d'être ombre entre les ombres, l'ombre qui viendra et reviendra dans ta vie ensoleillé

I have dreamed vividly of you—I have walked with, spoken to, loved your shadow so often and so much that nothing else remains of you—nothing remains for me but to be a shadow among shadows, the shadow who will come and come again into your sun-drenched life

—Robert Desnos

I

August 1987: In my early thirties I decided certain things about my life. Two years earlier I'd bailed out of a relationship with a kindhearted, thoughtful man—a fine companion for summer days and winter nights, but not a life partner. I'd spent the intervening time in desultory dating, but opportunities for romance don't present themselves often to writers, introverted curmudgeons who work at home. More to the point, everywhere I turned I encountered the inexorable law of desire: those whom I wanted didn't want me; those who wanted me I didn't want.

Enough such hopeless affairs and I decided this: single, childless, I would close up emotional shop, to put myself out into the world and see where it might take me. I was thirty-four and aging as fast as the rest of us; I needed to spend some time alone, letting my heart repair itself. I packed up my meager belongings and stored them in a friend's basement. I arranged to house-sit for a friend, to be followed by a residency at a nearby artists' colony. I'd spend the year floating and writing. I turned my back on love.

A month later Larry Rose entered my life.

Romance and sleep, in this they are alike: Each arrives only when you're looking the other way.

We met at the reception following the memorial service for a former roommate of mine (as so often happens: Death provides humus for love). At the time I was catering to my worst instincts by flirting with a lawyer with whom I associated money, intellectual prowess, power; all the requirements, I thought then, for true love.

The lawyer placed his hand on my arm. "I really enjoy talking with you. Maybe we should get together sometime."

"Sure," I said. "Let me give you my phone number."

He took my number, tucked it in his pocket, and produced a business card. "Sometime soon." Then he glanced across the room. "Oh, if you'll excuse me. I have to go check with my boyfriend."

I watched him go. I turned around to find Larry at my side.

A letter to a friend:

> Dear B.,
>
> I went to an old roommate's memorial service on Saturday and met two guys—a lawyer whom I'm really attracted to, and a Berkeley High School English teacher named Larry Rose, who's really attracted to me. So I came home and placed this bet with myself: The phone will ring on Tuesday, and it will be the Berkeley High English teacher.

The phone rang Monday, and it was Larry.

We made a weeknight dinner date. I met him at a restaurant—I can't remember what kind, American or ethnic or continental, and this frustrates me; I remember only that it was small and crowded. Knowing Larry, it was probably good and possibly French. This will have to do.

Even in my thirties I saw restaurants as foreign territories, where I was an easily intimidated tourist. I'd grown up in rural Kentucky, where I'd seldom ordered from a menu; eating out had been a novelty, restricted to occasional trips to the burger joint in the county seat. My vast family ate meals prepared by my mother and sisters, featuring garden-grown vegetables, and meat that often as not my father had shot on the hoof or fish we'd pulled from the river. When I faced a packed restaurant with a waiting list, my first impulse was always to flee.

I searched for a corner where Larry and I might wait out the line. I located a couple of chairs and went back to find him.

He was chatting with the owner. "How is your wife?" Larry was asking. "Of course I remember her, she is so pretty! And your children, how are they?" While they talked, the owner was leading us deeper into the restaurant. I drew up the rear, until we found ourselves at a table for two tucked in a corner. As he shook hands with the owner, Larry proffered a bill.

"You didn't tell me you knew the owner," I said as we sat.

"I don't," Larry said. "How about starting with some oysters?"

"No, thanks. I cower before any raw creature."

Dinner conversation: We spoke of reading, art, and Europe, where he went every summer, from where he'd just returned. "Brittany has the greatest oysters," he said. "They sell them in big vats, right at the shore." He offered me a shell.

"Oh, I'll try anything once." It was, after all, a first date, and I didn't want to lose the possibility of romance over a bite of slimy mollusk. I gulped it down. It tasted like wind off the ocean, clean and pure and with a salty edge.

He took up another. "*Ma vie en rose.*"

I ventured a second oyster. "I speak some French."

His face lit up, and he plunged into rapid-fire conversation, until after a minute I held up my hand. "Maybe I should say I *used* to speak French. I studied it in college, but I've lost almost all of it."

"You'll pick it back up fast enough." He took up his tableware, fork in left hand, knife in right. From some distant conversation I remembered a friend's comment: exotic as a foreign lover.

But I remembered my resolve: no attachments; let the heart recuperate. During dinner I took care to speak of my plans for the future, making no mention of a partner. "I might not even be living here in a few years," I said. "I might be teaching at some junior college in the rural Midwest, I don't know. All that future stuff is up for grabs now." He nodded and kept eating. "And what about you?" I asked. "Are you happy teaching English? Could you imagine doing something different, living someplace else a few years from now?"

He shrugged. "I'm happy teaching. A few years from now I'll worry about a few years from now." He lifted his wineglass. "It's been awfully cool for this time of year."

At the end of the main course the waiter approached. "Would you like anything more?"

Larry commandeered the dessert menu. "That's what I like about France. In California the waiter asks, 'Would you like anything more?' In France they say, 'What will you have for dessert?' "

Afterward we squabbled over the check, that lovely ritual. I carefully divided the amount in half and left slightly more than my share before going to the men's room. When I returned, the check had been paid. Larry stuffed my money in my hip pocket. "You can pay next time."

At his door he invited me inside; I declined. "A school night," I said. "Let's stay in touch."

"Just remember you owe me dinner," he said.

Two weeks later I found myself in his bedroom.

In one corner a pile of dirty laundry crept up the wall. An ancient, dusty turntable sat atop the bureau. On the floor next to the bureau was stacked a waist-high pile of LPs (Bluebird-label jazz from the late 1940s and early 1950s, Donna Summer, Edith Piaf, Beethoven's Ninth, *The Magic Flute,* Aretha Franklin, Jim Morrison and the Doors). Some of the LPs had fallen into the piled laundry. Several of the bureau drawers protruded, revealing their innards: dozens of bars of soap; dozens of pairs of underwear; hundreds of batteries, most still shrink-wrapped and long past their expiration dates. Candles. All varieties of deodorants. Shaving creams. Condoms. Toothbrushes. Sunscreen. Hand lotion. Several traveling clocks—some ticking, some dead. HIV-awareness pamphlets. A slim volume of selected Shakespeare sonnets. All-male porn paper-backs in French, whose covers promised a cross between Barbara Cartland and Jean Genet. A large grocery bag filled with coins of various European currencies. London theater programs from the early 1980s. Dozens of unmatched socks.

What a slob, I thought.

An ebony black cat walked in, stepping familiarly around the piles of LPs and scattered cassettes, stirring a few lemon-sized dustballs from under the bed. He curled into a hollow he'd made for himself (a week ago? a month ago?) in the dirty laundry. "Allow me to present Willy," Larry said, bowing. "The little beast."

Sex for the first time: It was okay, not great; as safe as it's possi-ble to be and still dignify the act with a name. As Larry turned to remove his shirt, I studied his back and wondered, *Will I ever do this again with this man? Some visceral part of me complained: He has too many moles. He has love handles. He wears cologne.*

I hate cologne.

He turned around to survey me, lying on his bed. He made a frame with the fingers of both hands and caught me in it. "Boy, am I lucky," he said.

Careful, I thought. *This man wants to fall in love.*

He excused himself to the bathroom. I seized the chance to snoop in his life.

I was impressed by his bookshelves—packed to overflowing with English and American literature, as well as major works in the original language by German and French writers. I was put off by the clutter of his closet, the piebald mountain of dirty laundry. I crossed the room and checked out his bureau. Next to the dusty turntable sat at least ten bottles of expensive French colognes.

He returned sooner than I expected, to catch me inspecting the colognes. "Oh, I got those in France. You want to try some?"

"I'm not much on cologne," I said, but already he'd picked up a bottle and dabbed some on the inside of my wrist. "My favorite," he said. "Vetiver."

On our next date we sat outdoors, on the deck of a friend's place where I was house-sitting. We looked over the city, on one of those twice-a-year San Francisco nights when the night is something close to warm. We sat in shorts and watched the city's lights come on, with all the life and hope they imply.

He told me the bare outlines of his parents' stories—German Jews, they'd fled separately to Holland in the 1930s. There they met through friends, but shortly later were trapped by the Nazi invasion. As Jews in occupied Holland, they were unable to marry; eventually Larry's father was imprisoned, then released, then imprisoned and beaten, then released again, this time with broken vertebrae. Unable to obtain medical care, he took Kathy and went into hiding. For almost three years they lived in an unheated second-floor room in a small town near the German border; then liberation, back surgery for Larry's father, marriage, and emigration to Los Angeles. Larry had been born a year after they arrived.

Listening, I thought, *This man has a history. This man has grown from some fertile sorrow.*

But I saw that already he was growing attached. I placed my hand on his bare knee and gave that famous speech, impossible to make new or original. I like you a lot but, I said. I'm not ready to get involved. I've decided to be alone for a while. We can keep dating if you want. If not, let's be friends.

He considered this. "There's something you ought to know," he said. In the mid-1980s, in San Francisco, among gay men there could be only one thing I ought to know, and I'd sensed it already. A delicate vacancy around the edges of words; his careful and limited use of the future tense; my intuition that my particular life script called for me to be taught some lesson by love, and my knowledge that such learning often comes hard.

He spoke the terrible facts aloud—HIV-positive, still healthy, no symptoms, T-cell count still high, above 800, almost normal.

He had yet to tell his parents because, after all, they were aged, who could know what might come to pass. In the silence that followed I thought, *At least I spoke first; at least I can't be accused, I can't accuse myself of leaving him because he is infected.*

To many people my guilt seems crazy. We'd known each other barely a month, hardly long enough for substantial commitment. What more sensible reason to reject a lover than the revelation of a terminal, communicable disease?

I can give a few rational answers to the question. At the time I didn't know whether I myself was HIV-positive or HIV-negative. I saw no surer way to tempt fate than to reject someone because he was seropositive, when I myself might be carrying the virus. More to the point, I was innocent of death. I did not understand the substance of his words, the death toward which they pointed. I'd sat with my father when he died, but he was an old man, his death had come as the merciful end to a prolonged illness. I felt no connection between that experience and this moment, sitting on this warm night with this man who was beginning to penetrate my defenses—already I was noticing the affection with which he spoke of his parents, his warmth in speaking of his students, the swell of his biceps defined by his short-sleeved shirt. He was getting to me, on this warm night when it was impossible to conceive of him as other than who he was—thick-muscled, barrel-chested, filled with desire for more: more dessert, more life, more me.

Lesson one of the geography of the heart: how love chooses us, if we will let it, rather than the other way around.

I continued to see him. No—I let him court me. He brought flowers—not your garden-variety carnations and mums, but fabulous arrangements of tropical flora with unpronounceable names and big hair. He telephoned, often enough that I looked forward to his calls; not so often as to annoy. He went for broke.

I held out.

We went to the gym in those days—he to preserve his health, and from vanity; I from vanity. We were princes among men, old enough to have grown into our bodies, young enough to be innocent of our beauty. Like many gay men, we'd been scrawny bookworms well into our twenties, only then to discover our bodies with surprise and pleasure.

He owned a good camera, and he delighted in taking pictures, mostly of me. In one photo he has posed me sprawled on a couch, bare-chested, wearing partly unbuttoned 501s and around my bare neck a tie, picked up in some secondhand store—silk, Brooks Brothers, knotted in a Windsor but punkish; narrow, black, flecked with white squares. It drapes along the swell of my chest, following the curve of my pectoral, lending an illusion of depth. He has made me hook my right arm up and back and over my head to display that most seductive of male lines, the steep, shallow S formed as the pectoral muscle flows upward, its horizontal curve merging into the biceps' vertical swell. The basilar vein glows blue through my translucent flesh.

I am thick with lust. My eyes hold no knowledge of loss or death. I will never grow old. No one, nothing I love will ever die.

And Larry: What a body. No, not a flawless body. His fondness for all things French (*tartes aux framboises,* Roquefort, pâté) revealed itself at his waistline. His nails were splotched with white, in what I later learned was an early sign of a compromised immune system. He towered over his parents, but at five feet eight inches he was four inches shorter than I.

But he had his father's hair, thick and full and running to rich, luxurious waves when it grew long, and his father's eyes, the thin blue of sky before clouds. He had the chest of a bodybuilder, though he was no gym fanatic; one glance at barbells and his muscles thickened. (No one under forty will believe, says Kate Vaiden in Reynolds Price's novel of the same name, how much everything is a matter of what's in the blood. No one, that is, who's not tried for the sake of vanity to alter body type.)

As undershirts he wore sleeveless singlets in the style of basketball players or track stars. I struck up the ritual of ripping them from his chest. In a photograph I took that same evening he stands in his underwear, his undershirt half-torn and dangling by one strap from his shoulder; what remains of the shirt drapes across his chest. In an effort to play butch he's clenched his jaw and tightened his eyes—the effect is less of ferocity than of profound sadness. Looking at these photos, I wonder how much he ever forgot his illness; how much he concealed it from me—partly to sustain hope, partly to protect me from his worry, partly from fear that if I saw too much of his fear, I'd bail out.

A few months into this relationship, I could easily have bailed out. We both knew this. I took care to remind him of it, in ways more and less subtle. "We could have a great time on a vacation in France," he'd say. "I'm not sure what I'm doing this summer," I'd say. And so on—he testing, I holding back.

Son of Holocaust survivors, Larry bought French shirts, Italian sweaters, vintage wines for daily suppers; he inherited a passion for the moment that his HIV status only intensified. Son of Depression survivors, I hoarded the last bit of soap, carefully sticking it to its succeeding bar. If I'd considered death at all, it was as a dark cloud on someone else's horizon; even my father's death a few years earlier had done little to shake my assumption of my own immortality. I was a white man in America, not rich but with no wolves anywhere near the door. My bent sexuality gave me insight into some way of being other than boundless American optimism, but for many years I'd lived in California and I'd acquired the prevailing denial of darkness and death. There was, of course, the issue of my own, unknown HIV status, but I'd managed to tuck that into some obscure pigeonhole of the mind. Then I met Larry.

I'd never encountered someone so immediately present. While I was paying attention to next year's rent, he slipped into my life with the force and immediacy of the here and now. Without my knowing it, our two ways of being engaged each other—my preoccupation with the future; his immersion in this day, this hour, this minute.

He bought gifts for every occasion and no occasion. Each gift arrived wrapped in designer paper pretty enough to frame. For my birthday, two months after our first meeting, he gave me a large box. He watched with growing impatience as I opened the package, slipping my finger under the Scotch tape, pulling open the end flaps, smoothing the paper over my knees. "Come *on*," he said, "*open* the damn thing, for God's sake."

I folded the paper into a neat square. "You never know when you'll need a piece of store-bought wrapping paper. Besides, I like to prolong the suspense."

Inside was a thick wool sweater, a medium blue with complex geometric patterns woven in cobalt. I understood what it represented. "You can't give me something so expensive," I said.

"Really, it wasn't that expensive."

I looked at him, held the sweater up, displayed its Italian label. "Right."

"It was on sale."

"Larry."

"Look, it's your birthday."

"If I take presents like this from you, if I let you buy me such things, then I feel like I have to give you something like this in return. And to put it bluntly, I can't afford to."

"I don't care."

"I know you don't care. For better or worse, *I* care."

We faced off for a short, silent moment, while I considered what to do. I had resolved to be alone for a while; he was pushing against that resolution.

Refusing the sweater would be ungracious, of course. (Besides, I wanted it.) But accepting it meant commitment, or at least a more painful breakup from this deepening involvement with an HIV-positive man. Larry, I would discover, was well aware of the implications of his generosity, and more than capable of using it as a means to the end of getting what he wanted.

I gave him a kiss. "Okay, but no more presents, not for a while, okay?"

"Okay. A little while."

I tried on the sweater and admired it.

"Oh," he said. "My doctor called to give me my latest T-cell count. Seven hundred and fifty."

"But you can lose a hundred here and there just from a cold. You had a cold last week."

"A bad cold."

I took the sweater off.

"He's mentioned a new drug," he said. "Something called AZT. It looks promising."

"Right."

The night after the news of his falling T-cell count, I awoke to his mumbling, an incoherent, stumbling stream of words. I placed a hand on his arm. At my touch he leapt up with a shriek, trembling with fear. He was dreaming, he said, that his parents had not escaped Nazi Germany but were being carted to the ovens.

In my arms he went back to sleep. I lay awake until dawn, staring at the ceiling. "I can't take this," I finally said aloud. "I can't go through with it. Anyone would understand. Larry will understand."

A few nights later, we were preparing not for lovemaking but for bed, on some ordinary night when we both had to get up early. Lying in bed, I watched him tug his shirt over his head, and some part of me, the writer part of me, noticed what I was noticing: not his moles or his hint of love handles. Now I was seeing his thick biceps and thicker hair and the way in which he folded his shirt and laid it neatly atop the mounded heap of dirty laundry, a gesture that could be only for my benefit. I had never asked this of him. I had never commented on his chaotic apartment.

And still I would not let myself give in.

I allowed to pass what I considered a decent interval after accepting the sweater. Then I steeled myself. I could not lead him on; I had a responsibility to speak. I delivered that tired speech yet again: "You're getting too serious. It freaks me out. Let's go a few months without seeing each other. If it's meant to happen, we'll get back together."

He studied this a moment. "One month."

"Three months."

"Six weeks."

"Two months, and that's final," I said. "And don't call me, I'll call you."

And so I went about reclaiming a life without him, and this is what haunted me:

Those spiky floral arrangements. Racy paperbacks in French. Thank-you notes, in an unmannered era. His devotion to his teaching and his students. His devotion to his parents; his struggle to free himself from his parents.

And as much as these:

Sprawled in bed; spoons. He sleeps. I study the mottled expanse of his broad back. I work my hand under his right arm, under his armpit, across his chest, to wrap it around his upper left arm. His biceps and triceps rest against the quilt, flattened by gravity. I stretch my large hand—my long fingers reach and fail to encompass his biceps, this thick hock of muscle, and at their failure my belly contracts, the lake of desire turns over. He stirs. The muscles of his back ripple. He turns over to face me.

What is this desire that seizes us in its fist to drag us in its wake?

Six weeks passed. I called him. He brought flowers.

There is something subversive in a man carrying flowers.

II

I was lying in bed with my back to the door, wearing my underwear as a nightcap—a bad joke of the kind Larry adored. He entered, grabbed his camera, took a picture.

Without turning over I raised my arm and pointed to the bed. "It's a school night. Come to bed."

He whipped the underwear from my head and tossed it on the covers. "I want to read you something."

If I turned over, time would do its lovemaking thing and it would be an hour and a half later and we'd still be awake. "It's late," I said. "You have to teach tomorrow. I have a long day ahead of me. Come. To. Bed."

"It's not too long. It's my favorite poem."

I sighed and turned over, hiding the underwear in one hand to fling at him when I caught him unawares.

" 'Eve of St. Agnes.' By John Keats."

"*Keats,*" I groaned. I threw the underwear at him. "I thought you said this was short."

"Hey, you started all this," he said, and he was right. Over supper and in the car I'd been reading aloud whatever I found interesting and asked him to do the same, but this was the first of many nights when we'd read to each other in bed.

Keats, the passionate poet dead at twenty-five, tells the story of the lover Porphyro, searching for a way to win his beloved Madeline, whose family will not allow them to marry. On the coldest night of the year, Madeline prepares herself for sleep according to the St. Agnes' Eve rituals, which promise to bring her a vision of her life's true love.

They told her how, upon St. Agnes' Eve,
Young virgins might have visions of delight,
And soft adorings from their loves receive
Upon the honeyed middle of the night,
If ceremonies due they did aright;
As, supperless to bed they must retire,
And couch supine their beauties, lily white;
Nor look behind, nor sideways, but require
Of Heaven with upward eyes for all that they desire.

Porphyro bribes his way into Madeline's bedroom and conceals himself behind a curtain. As she's waking from her dreams, he reveals himself and takes her hand.

Let us away, my love, with happy speed;
There are no ears to hear, or eyes to see . . .
Awake! arise! my love, and fearless be,
For over the southern moors I have a home
    for thee. . . .

And they are gone: aye, ages long ago
These lovers fled away into the storm.

Larry closed the book. " 'Awake! arise! my love, and fearless be,' " he said, but I was half-asleep. No fleeing that night, or any time soon.

III

After World War II Fred and Kathy, Larry's parents, had few connections left in Europe. Most of Fred's family had long ago emigrated to southern California. Shortly after he fled Germany, he had divorced his first wife, with whom he'd had two daughters. He arranged false identification papers for all three, enabling them to survive the war, but he was trapped by the German blitzkrieg invasion of Holland and by his refusal to leave Kathy. After the Nazi takeover of Amsterdam, she'd been among the first to receive orders to report to a German labor camp. Fred arranged a place for her to hide, then a year later moved with her to a small town near the German border, where they hid until the Allied liberation three years later. They emerged to learn that Kathy's parents and sister had died in concentration camps.

After Fred's back surgery, he and Kathy married in Amsterdam, then emigrated as displaced persons to join his relatives in the capital of dreams: Los Angeles in the late 1940s. Fred was almost fifty, Kathy almost forty; they spoke no English, they had little money. Before the rise of the Nazis forced his flight to Holland, Fred had been president of a bank. Now he and Kathy took their first jobs, which they located through their milkman: working as gardener and housekeeper for Art Linkletter.

They left their jobs with the Linkletters soon enough. Fred lived in chronic pain; even after surgery, his back would not allow him to do yard work. For a while he bought shoes wholesale, to sell on the street to returning GIs. Kathy continued working as a housekeeper. Within a year of their arrival in America, she gave birth to Larry.

He was a difficult birth—born prematurely, he weighed barely three pounds and spent the first weeks of his life in an incubator, perilously close to death. His struggle to survive must have rendered him more precious to parents themselves so recently delivered from war and destruction.

At home and between themselves Fred and Kathy spoke German; with their son they spoke fractured English, which he soon grew old enough to correct. They spent their days establishing a place for themselves (middle-aged, foreigners, survivors) in a new country. At night their world centered around their only child.

I was born ninth of nine children in the Kentucky knobs, a westward-flung, northwest-curling finger of the Appalachians; steep, Catholic-ridden ridges that form a ragged barrier between the ruling-class Baptists and gentleman-farmer Presbyterians of the rolling Bluegrass (to the north and east) and the foot-washing Baptists and dirt-poor Pentecostals of the lumpy Pennyrile (to the south and west). Across nearly two centuries, the Catholics of the knobs made a living servicing vice, our own and our neighbors'. In spring and summer, when creeks ran full in their limestone beds, distilleries ran round the clock. Men farmed tobacco during the day, then worked the night shift making bourbon at Jim Beam, Seagram, Heaven Hill. Women raised kids in daylight, then worked the bottling plants at night. In fall the creeks ran low, the distilleries shut down, and we turned to the tobacco harvest. Men hung leaves from the rafters of slit-sided curing barns; women sat at long tables tying leaves into bunches, called hands.

When your living is tied to sin, you tend toward a liberal view on the subject, a fact our Protestant neighbors appreciated. Over the years my town became an ecumenical melting pot, a place to practice vice, where (according to my father) you could tell a man's religion by his weapon, or lack of one. Catholics carried guns, Baptists carried knives, Presbyterians stayed in their cars and used the drive-up window—invented, at my family's tavern anyway, to service the demands of their propriety.

Early on the morning of my birth my mother felt the first labor pains. She put on a deer roast (onions to chop and fry, meat to dredge in flour and braise, carrots and potatoes to peel). She organized my seven brothers and sisters (one child had died in infancy) to go to Sunday mass.

With the kids and my father off to church, my mother got in the car to drive herself sixteen miles to the hospital, whose antiseptic rooms and bland meals she looked forward to as a luxury. She'd delivered her first babies at home, where household demands had her up and about almost before the baby stopped its first cries. Hospitals she saw as well-earned R&R.

But I was impatient, then as now. Three miles down the road my mother realized that I was coming faster than fifty miles an hour. She pulled into the driveway of her doctor—aged Dr. Mudd, distantly related to the doctor who had treated John Wilkes Booth and nearly his contemporary. He gave her a sedative to knock her out (to this day she complains that this spoiled my delivery). Then he drove her to the hospital, where he delivered me at 11 A.M. Ten solid pounds: more than a roasting chicken, less than a turkey (though not by much).

Of years filled with terror and death, Larry's father spoke almost exclusively of joy and life. Fred had endured the great traumas of modern history: the First World War; the financial, political, and social collapse of Germany in the 1920s; the rise of Hitler; flight to Holland; the Second World War, with its years of hiding. Then emigration as a displaced person to America, and the brave new world of a wildly expanding Los Angeles in the 1950s. Twice history had laid waste his life: first when he fled to Holland, second when he and his future wife went into hiding. Each time he fought his way back to prosperity.

Elegant in his dark suit and tie, sitting on the couch in his Santa Monica living room with the latest in a series of beloved schnauzers at his feet, Fred spoke good if heavily accented English—he had not spoken a word of it prior to emigrating to America. Occasionally and unconsciously he slipped into German, and I glimpsed for a moment another person—some part of his first, lost life.

These were the stories of his long life that he related to Larry and to me late in Larry's life, after I'd been accepted into the family; this was what he allowed himself to speak of and pass on:

At fourteen, a teenager in a small northern German town, he ran to the train station with his mother to see off Kaiser Wilhelm's soldiers, departing Germany for the battlefields of World War I. With all the women of the village, his mother made baskets of sandwiches, which Fred helped her thrust into the soldiers' overburdened hands. There were so many women thrusting out sandwiches that the soldiers passed them back to feed to their horses, penned in boxcars behind the passenger compartments.

Two years later Fred was pulled from high school and sent to the orchards to pick apples—no adult men remained to do the job. Now the trains returned from the French fronts, but they passed through the village in the night, so as to conceal their freight loads of dead and wounded.

Throughout the 1920s and into the 1930s Fred worked his way upward in banking and finance, eventually assuming the presidency of a bank in a small town near Düsseldorf. With the rise of the Nazis he was driven from that position; shortly afterward he fled to Holland. There he used his position as a trader in foreign currencies to funnel gentile clients' money into the bank accounts of emigrating Jews. He left it there long enough to establish the emigrants' wealth to the satisfaction of American immigration officials; then, once the Jews were safely embarked, Fred restored the money to its original, unsuspecting owners' accounts. With Kathy still in Holland, he refused to emigrate. He helped her into hiding.

He spoke of the morning of the German invasion of Amsterdam, when he sat on the balcony of his apartment, looking down on the ranks of passing Nazi soldiers. A professor who lived next door rushed into his apartment imploring, What's to be done? The professor spoke of suicide. Fred shrugged. "Have some coffee," he said, and offered a cup.

He talked very little and then with reluctance of his two imprisonments, or the beating in which Nazis broke his back. He was uncertain why they released him from prison—he speculated that his loud and frequent references to his Swiss brother-in-law may have helped, as Switzerland was Germany's essential financial connection to the world outside Europe, and the Nazis were wary of any scandal that might alienate the Swiss.

He located Kathy. Together they fled Amsterdam, buying their way into a single room on the second floor of a small house near the German border. "We thought we would be there a month or two," he said. For almost three years they lived in that room, eating what food their protectors were able to spare. For most of that time Fred was confined to bed by his broken back, for which he could not seek treatment.

A neighbor warned them that the Nazis were searching houses for Jews, one of many searches the neighborhood endured. Their landlady formulated a plan: She would pretend to be ill and would take to bed; Kathy would dress as a nurse and sit at her side. They would stuff Fred, broken back notwithstanding, into the minuscule crawl space under the floorboards.

Lying in bed, waiting for the Nazis to arrive, the landlady prayed aloud to her statue of St. Anthony, patron of lost causes. If Fred and Kathy were not discovered, if she herself was not taken by the police, she promised to give five guldens to the church in St. Anthony's name. Sitting at her side, Kathy spoke up. "Ten guldens." From under the floorboards Fred called, "Fifty guldens!" After the war he returned to make good his promise.

After the war: An indomitable entrepreneur, Fred cornered the concession for wine, the first wine to be sold to the Dutch public after liberation. Standing at canalside, he was watching a crane lift a cask of wine to a warehouse. In midair the barrel slipped from its trusses and crashed to the street. The wine puddled in the gutters. People lay on the cobblestones to lap it up. "What could I do?" Fred asked as he told this story. "I laughed."

After naming eight children my parents had run out of ideas for names, so they turned me over for naming to the monks at the nearby Trappist monastery of Our Lady of Gethsemane, the rural Kentucky abbey where Thomas Merton wrote. In the 1950s the Trappists more rigidly observed the rule of silence and mortification of the flesh. They spoke only at prayer or in emergency; they slept on pallets in unheated rooms; they fasted on not much more than bread and water throughout Lent and on all Fridays. My father, a maintenance worker at a local Seagram distillery, delivered to the monastery the bourbon the monks used in the fruitcakes they baked and sold to raise money. The monks appreciated my father's studied casualness in counting the bottles; for his part my father preferred their company to the responsibilities of parenting his sprawling brood. Within months of their acquaintance, some of those monks became regulars at our dining table.

The monks elected to name me after their baker, an Irish-American who on entering the monastery had been assigned the name of Fintan, a ninth-century Irish abbot. My mother, a Protestant convert not especially well versed in Irish hagiography, misspelled the name on my birth certificate.

Fintan honored me royally, concocting elaborate cakes for each of my birthdays. In a photograph taken on my fourth birthday I'm posed with a cake made in the shape of Mickey Mouse's head—rendered with painstaking verisimilitude in vanilla and chocolate icing, Mickey is almost as large as I.

That photograph evokes an era in which our lives became intertwined with those of the monks. Throughout my childhood, using various subterfuges, the monks slipped from the abbey to make their way to our house, managing to arrive just before supper. *They* got pork chops, *we* got fried baloney, but still as children we adored their company. For the most part they were educated men, Yankees from impossibly exotic places (Cleveland, Detroit), who stayed late into the evening drinking beer, smoking cigarettes, watching football on television, and talking, talking, talking.

Brother A. was fond of a fake grass skirt someone had sent my mother from Hawaii. When the moon was right and the whiskey flowing, he donned the skirt and some hot-pink plastic leis, then hoisted my mother to the tabletop and climbed up after. There she sang "Hard-Hearted Hannah" ("the vamp of Savannah, G-A!"), while Brother A. swayed his hips and and waved his hands in mock hula. Later he launched into Broadway tunes, warbling in falsetto with his arms thrown around one or more of his brethren. As for Brother Fintan, he was a party boy at heart, a jack monk who vanished from the monastery when I was five, for reasons I wouldn't figure out for many years.

At eight years old, Larry saw a fishing program on television. Immediately he had to go fishing—the famous fishing expedition. He would not be satisfied until he was sitting on a riverbank, pole in hand, however he might live in suburban Los Angeles, with the nearest fishable river somewhere in the southern California mountains. Fred had never seen a fish swimming in anything but butter-and-lemon sauce, but he obligingly bought fishing poles and hooks, and together father and son drove to Laguna Beach, some fifty miles distant. Fred parked, found a pier, buckled himself and Larry into life vests, and stepped boldly into what was surely his first and last venture into the great American out-of-doors (albeit at the ocean).

They sat side by side at midpier. Fred had conveniently forgotten bait, a small detail, but Larry was not one to dwell on particulars. Before long they tossed their hooks over the edge, only to find their lines were too short. "We sat there with our bare hooks dangling a mile above the water," Larry told me. "I guess I should have felt like a fool, but in fact all I remember is feeling warm and secure and happy to be sitting at my father's side."

I grew up hungry to see the big city, which to me constituted any place with parallel parking. The rugged hills surrounding my Kentucky hometown had effectively kept civilization at bay until around 1960; in nearly two centuries only a few daring souls from either my mother's or father's families had moved more than a few miles away.

Then we began to acquire televisions. With everyone literally watching, television brought California to the knobs. With it came the turbulent 1960s, the first decade to reach us more or less on schedule.

My family acquired a black-and-white, hand-me-down television in a wood-grain case. On clear nights the signal was lost to the universe, but on overcast nights it bounced off the clouds and into our wide valley. On those nights we picked up fuzzy versions of NBC and CBS, but these were enough. NBC carried Walt Disney, and even in this two-hundred-year-old town of eight hundred people buried in the Kentucky knobs, he had his impact. It would be a cloudy Sunday evening, and the fields that stretched along the east side of the Jackson Highway would be swarming with kids playing fox and hounds and kick the can, and then it would be seven-thirty and we would disappear all at once, to our houses, or to the houses of neighbors rich enough to own televisions, to watch *Walt Disney's Wonderful World of Color* in black and white.

Courtesy of television, I came to think of the *Wonderful World of Color* as synonymous with California. Walter Cronkite broadcast from New York, but the gray walls of his newsroom might be anywhere; there was no mistaking the whereabouts of Disneyland. I saw the streets of endless suburbia, lined with orange trees and washed eternally with sunshine. I saw surfers under palm trees, whose pointy fronds hinted at moonlit frolics on the beach. I saw images of a bucolic countryside where city boys speaking high English led adventurous lives with heroic pets, where smart city folks brought enlightenment and progress to ignorant farmers.

And more: I watched *The Beverly Hillbillies* and *Green Acres* and saw myself, or at least how television presented me to the world. I watched and then went outside, to see my knobs in a new light: swarming with mosquitoes and smartweed, peopled with yokels, demanding everlasting labor to produce not oranges and melons and the glamour of Hollywood, but demon booze and tobacco, that evil weed. I watched and compared and, through television, came to know both shame and envy.

California! I dreamed of it on my school bus, kids packed three to a seat and in the aisles. The route wound through hills populated by white people whose surnames relegated them from birth to peeling clapboard shacks with tin roofs. The kids from the hollers had no running water, and around January the bus got rank; across February and March I cultivated the habit of taking a deep breath before climbing aboard. In the county seat, black children were crammed onto an already crowded bus, adding racial tension to the overburdened air. When I could, I grabbed a window seat and looked out, dreaming of a place where there was no racism, no poverty, hot water for all, and no sweat after a day's work; dreaming, in a word, of California.

Kathy and Fred had been in America several years when the West German government began to pay reparations to Jews who had lost family and property in the Holocaust. Partly with the help of this money, they rented space and opened a small department store. Eventually, in the way of so many American immigrants, they bought the store, then rented it to a family of Vietnamese, another of this country's refugees from distant wars.

When Larry was eleven, they took him back to Europe, where they visited the Anne Frank house in Amsterdam—set up not unlike the room where Kathy and Fred had themselves gone into hiding. They thought it important that Larry know his Jewish heritage.

At the same time they took care to immerse Larry in all they perceived as American, especially the glitz and glamour of nearby Hollywood. So it came to pass that he was standing with Kathy at the back of a crowded television studio, for what he later told me was the first filming of *The Lucy Show*. July 19, 1962: In his neat, rounded hand Larry (he of the eidetic memory) noted the date in the brown leatherette autograph book that I found among his effects and that sits before me as I write.

The studio lights dimmed. Lucy's mother swept through the audience, followed by a retinue of relatives, friends, groupies. Thirteen-year-old Larry stepped forward to thrust out his autograph book. Flattered, Mrs. Ball ("Desiree, to you") waved Larry and his mother to the front. As she ushered them into first-row seats, she leaned over to whisper in Larry's ear. "It's not what you know, it's who you know," she said, and winked. The band struck up the theme. For the next several years, with a faithfulness that in my thoroughly Catholic childhood was reserved for the affairs of God, Larry and his mother attended *The Lucy Show*'s every filming, seated at the right hand of Desiree Ball.

Around the studio lots Larry encountered the stars of the day, and soon he approached them with his brown leatherette autograph book. Who could resist the entreaty of this impeccably well-mannered boy, accompanied by an evidently displaced mother still struggling with her *w*'s? Not, judging from Larry's autograph book, Maurice Chevalier (a Gallic flourish underscores a florid execution), Dick Van Dyke, Jay North ("Dennis the Menace"), Sammy Davis Jr. (the pen all over the page), Jack Benny (a pinched, parsimonious hand), Clint Eastwood (uncertain of his fame, he takes care to append his TV name—"Rowdy"). And of course there were *The Lucy Show* players, as well as assorted hangers-on—Vivian Vance, Desi Arnaz IV, Bill Frawley, Richard Keith ("Little Ricky"), Lucy herself.

Ella Fitzgerald. Hedda Hopper. Natalie Wood, unaware of her watery fate. Count Basie. "Lorna" ("Judy Garland's daughter"—Larry's careful note). Julieta Shansy—Miss Brazil 1962, attending the International Beauty Congress (at thirteen years old, what was Larry *doing* at the International Beauty Congress?). Pierre Salinger. Pat Brown. Zubin Mehta, whom Larry surprised (he told me) postperformance in his dressing room, shirtless and dripping with sweat.

As I page through the book, snapshots fall out: Larry on a red-letter day at the Santa Anita racetrack, posed at the side of Allen Ludden, Ann Sothern, and Eve Arden (two-piece, avocado green suit, Buster Brown collar, sunglasses removed for the photo). Clipped to the snapshots, a tomato sauce–stained cocktail napkin with Pearl Bailey's signature scrawled across its corner—a relic of Larry's days of haunting the Brown Derby, where he and his mother badgered the maître d' into seating them near the rich and famous.

Or the less prosperous and lesser known. Who is Wilbur Hatch? Mina Martinez? Ziva Rodann, Perc Westmore? Larry, a polite boy, evidently requested all the signatures at the table, however he might want only Miss Bailey's. Immortality comes easy to the lunch companions of the big-time stars.

Not that he limited his autograph grubbing to the Brown Derby and the Desilu back lots.

> 20th April, 1960.
> I am commanded by the Queen to write and thank you
> for your letter, and for the congratulations which you
> sent to Her Majesty on the birth of her baby.
>
> I have to explain to you that, owing to Her Majesty's
> rules in these matters, The Queen does not send auto-
> graphs to people with whom she is not already person-
> ally acquainted.
> Susan Mussey, Lady-in-Waiting.

16th November, 1961.
I have received the Queen's command to thank you
most sincerely for your kind message of good wishes
to The Prince of Wales on the occasion of His Royal
Highness's birthday.

Susan Mussey, Lady-in-Waiting.

25th April, 1962.
The Queen has commanded me to thank you for the
message of good wishes which you have so kindly sent
on the occasion of Her Majesty's birthday.

Susan Mussey, Lady-in-Waiting.

There are probably two dozen of these notes, each slightly more
brusque than its predecessor, most under the signature of the
patient Susan Mussey; Larry was nothing if not persistent.

All but one of his famous addressees sent canned responses
cranked out and signed by flunkies. Herbert Hoover; Jacqueline
Kennedy on the occasion of her son's birth; Robert Kennedy;
Eugene McCarthy; Jacqueline Kennedy on the occasion of her mis-
carriage; Pope John XXIII; Jacqueline Kennedy on the occasion of
her husband's assassination—none of these notes was signed by the
real McCoy, but in an era before computers or photocopy
machines, each is flawlessly, manually typed. The image comes
helplessly to mind: a thousand Susan Musseys at a thousand Smith-
Corona typewriters, banging out kind notes of rejection to a
world of thirteen-year-olds seeking an authentically signed note—
from the Queen, from the Pope, from Jackie on the occasion of
her various misfortunes.

Chaff and more chaff, until buried in this haystack of chaff I
find the needle, the payoff of Larry's persistence. Amid this flood
of form letters arrived a personal response written on personal
stationery from a man of the old school, a Frenchman (of course)
bound by duty and manners, who understood that all personal

correspondence is to be answered personally. And so in response to Larry's sympathies on the occasion of his gallbladder surgery, writing in his own hand from his office as *président de la république* (the *république* where twenty-six years later Larry will greet his death):

> *30 avril 1964.*
> *Très sensible à votre aimable pensée. Je vous en remercie de tout coeur.*
>
> Charles de Gaulle

> [30 April 1964.
> I'm touched by your kind thoughts. I send my warmest thanks.
>
> Charles de Gaulle]

My seventh grade began with Sister Marie Therese announcing that she would not teach math or science. These were godless subjects, she said, in which we'd be amply indoctrinated later on. *She* would give over those precious hours of instruction to penmanship and religion.

So my classmates and I filed to the front of the room, where we stacked our math and science books under the cyclopean eye of God, painted on the plaster above the blackboard—blue, of course, and slightly bloodshot, floating amid towering cumuli. The textbooks sat there through the year, a pile of forbidden fruit, while Sister Marie Therese combined her favorite subjects by setting the class to copying by hand the entire text of the Baltimore Catechism.

I see her prowling the aisles, a small, osteoporotic woman in the flowing black rayon voile of the Ursulines, with a downy lip and myopic eyes and a single short gray hair growing from a mole in the center of her chin. Always she kept one hand held flat against her ample chest, poised to strike a sharp chop to the back of the student she caught idling or chatting or inhabiting the world without a patron saint (she routinely beat a girl named Linda for carrying a "pagan name"). Her stooped back kept her in some small agony; from under her black robes peeked white tennis shoes, worn, we were sure, to facilitate her lightning attacks, but more likely because they were easier on her feet than the regulation low-heeled black pumps. Behind her back we called her B.C., a nickname coined in recognition of her age.

Fairness was not a concept for which she had much use. Like many Southern Catholics her theology was an odd mix of Baltimore Catechism and Americanized Calvinism: Justice was the Lord's, to be meted out mercilessly and in ways beyond human understanding; her teacher's role was to initiate us into an appreciation of our place as sinners in the hands of an angry God, a Protestant notion with which she was quite at home.

Over many years and much recounting of her tale, I begrudged her mightily that stack of unopened science books. Then shortly after Larry died, I'd known enough pain, my heart had enlarged itself enough, that I was given this revelation. I understood that Sister Marie Therese had refused to teach math and science because she could *not* teach math and science. In my rural village even the younger nuns had little formal training; B.C. had grown up an orphan on a remote western Kentucky farm, where she'd surely learned more about churning butter than Venn diagrams.

Sister Marie Therese would be saddened to learn how those afternoon-long sessions copying the Baltimore Catechism were the beginning of the deterioration of my penmanship. Saddened, but not surprised: She saw me as a troublemaker, this she established early in the year, when she caught me fabricating hundreds of variations on a wildly baroque signature, none of which resembled Palmer's cursive ideal.

By his own acknowledgment Larry had a happy childhood, even as he lived under a heavy burden of history, love, and expectation. Shortly after we met, I helped him learn to use a computer, so that he might begin to type a journal. He never got very far—he hadn't the obsession to be a writer, though equally to the point, he had no time; his life was consumed, first by his teaching and his devotion to his parents, later by his illness and his devotion to me.

But he wrote of his fear of abandonment, which arose from the mass and weight of his parents' histories and love.

I find it odd to be comfortable. Perhaps this is my greatest accomplishment, even though one could easily see my comfort as a liability instead. I tend to see it as a victory because part of me has always tended toward despair and panic, at the very least toward deep worry. . . . I recall a visit to the Claremont Colleges [seventy-five miles from his home] while in high school. The fact that I forgot part of my memorized oration against capital punishment and had to extemporize is nearly lost in my memory of that cold, gray, rainy day that would never end. The worst, by far, was my fear and conviction that I would never get home again, that I would never see my parents ever again. The problems loomed limitless and unsolvable. Would the car work? Would we (that is, myself and the school-associated people I was with) get in an accident? Would I catch cold and die? Would my parents die from worry about me? To say from my present perspective that these fears were wholly exaggerated and unnecessary does not change the intense reality that the experience had for me then.

. . . For me, growing up has been, more than anything, a matter of learning to trust in my ability to cope and to believe in the resiliency of both myself and my parents. No doubt, this issue relates back (at least in part) to my "memory" of the Holocaust. . . .

My basic view of the world was that it was rough and harsh and cruel and painful and risky except in the cocoon that my parents provided. For a part of me the point was merely to live, to survive. My handicap has been my illusion of being handicapped.

He wrote of how difficult he found it to break away from this "cocoon" of safety, how he clung to childhood until long after childhood because as long as he was taken care of, he was protected from engaging the world in all its cruelty. "I feigned innocence in order to have power," he wrote, a frank acknowledgment of his tendency to manipulate.

Later in his life he would live for months at a time in Europe, partly by way of exploring his European roots but partly by way of proving to himself that he could live apart from his parents. But he continued to accept their gifts of money; later he would be strongly drawn to me partly because I was so fiercely and wholly independent. As soon as he returned to America, he resumed his daily phone calls and monthly visits to Fred and Kathy—both easy enough to accomplish from San Francisco, but both an indication of the power of the ties that bound him to them. Among his journal entries:

How lucky I felt as a child to be in sunny California in the best country in the world. I used to collect weather statistics and I would study the life expectancies of earlier societies to appreciate how lucky I was. Moreover, how lucky I was to have such fine parents in such a fine house, etc., etc. But when it thundered or even rained hard so that I thought the thunder would come, I was terrified. I would rush to my parents' bed, where I felt sure I would be safe. Love would save me from all harm.

After my namesake Brother Fintan abruptly departed the monastery, I did not see him again until I was sixteen years old, when he returned for a New Year's Eve visit with my family, accompanied by a handsome young man.

From my earliest consciousness of my body I'd known I was drawn to men. At first this was merely puzzling, until I looked around and realized that no one I knew shared this powerful, growing thing. For some unknown reason I'd been visited with what I could see only as a curse—my religion was filled with tales of men and women whom demons singled out for temptation; I felt singled out in that way, except that where the saints always seemed confident that God was on their side, I was alone. Growing up gay in an isolated hill town, I never had so much as a hint that others might share my particular landscape of desire. By the time I was a teenager, this fact defined my interior life: the complete invisibility of any relevant model, good or bad, of passionate adult love.

I tried brainwashing myself—the only boy among the back rows reserved for the well-behaved students, I whiled away school days by imagining unspeakable acts with idealized women. This worked for a while, until I'd hear a distant rooster crow or the whistle of the midday L&N hurtling across a trestle. I'd be distracted for a split second, and when I returned to my ideal, I'd find she'd trans-formed herself into a hunky gymnast or a track star.

High school came; I tried dating girls. They liked going out with me because, one said, "I feel so safe," a confidence that depressed me for days. I wondered: What am I supposed to be feeling, and why can't I make it happen? In my quiet way I considered the books I'd read, the television shows and commercials I'd seen, my classmates' vocal heterosexuality. I decided passion was something other people felt. I concluded that I was an aberration, one of a kind, an emotional eunuch with a heart of stone.

Then Fintan and his companion appeared.

My family received them with its customary hospitality and enthusiasm and food and drink. More monks arrived to visit their old companion—there was dancing on the table; we trotted out the skirt and leis for Brother A., now in need of a stool to climb to the tabletop but otherwise as sinuous and campy as ever.

Afterward I listened for the customary postparty gossip. Had Fintan arrived with a woman, the household would have been abuzz: *Who is she? Might they get married?* Had he brought a mere friend, there would have been idle chatter: *Nice man. Needs a haircut.* But: Nothing. My namesake and his companion might never have sat at our table.

In my small town, among garrulous Southerners, only one subject invoked a silence so vast and deliberate. That night I went to bed understanding a great deal more about the world: the vastness of the gap between what we say and what we do; why Fintan had been asked to leave the monastery; the nature of his relationship with his handsome companion. In one night the world transformed itself into a very different place, one where I was not alone.

While Kathy was shepherding Larry to *The Lucy Show*, Fred was taking him to Chavez Ravine, to Los Angeles Dodgers games. Fred knew nothing of baseball; Larry, a studious boy, had no particular interest in it either. But like *The Lucy Show* filmings, this was an American ritual, whose green diamonds and peculiar rules held the promise of an American benediction. And so they went, father and son, the latest in an ongoing series of pilgrims seeking national identity in the stadium bleachers.

Shortly after his fourteenth birthday, Larry found his way postgame to the vicinity of the locker room—it was a different era, when persistent fans could come face-to-face with their idols. His leatherette autograph book offers a record of the day—the signatures of four Dodgers: Ron Gleason, Dick Nen, Joe Moeller, Pete Rickert. Mission accomplished, Larry looked about himself, to discover that in the crush of the crowd he'd been separated from his father.

He searched for a few minutes, then burst into tears, acutely conscious that he was too old to be bawling in public, yet consumed with the same unreasoning fear of abandonment and loss that in his journal he connected to his parents' Holocaust history. A Dodger Stadium employee spotted him crying and led him to the security office, where after an hour he was reunited with an anxious Fred.

At seventeen years old, after some desperate searching, I corralled a date for my high school senior prom. Neither I nor my parents could afford to fork out for rented togs, so I wore a tuxedo handed down from Mr. Barry, our next-door neighbor. He'd bought it used in the 1920s, when he and a group of World War I veterans played in a traveling roadhouse band called Paul and His Privates.

Mr. Barry's coat, shirt, and tie fit well enough, but the tuxedo pants hit me at midcalf. My resourceful mother improvised: She took a pair of my father's darkest pants (which fit me, more or less) and basted a strip of black mourning ribbon down each outside seam. I was humiliated, furious at this makeshift hand-me-down, until I arrived at the prom to discover that amid the pink, baby blue, and lime green tuxedos of the early 1970s, with their frilled plackets and matching polyester pants, the elegant black gabardine of Paul and His Privates was a hit, the envy of my classmates. Unwittingly I'd stumbled onto black as a fashion statement. Unwittingly I'd stumbled onto fashion, a notion I would not revisit until I met Larry.

But I would not meet Larry for many years—I'd not yet even

arrived at the prom. Instead I was standing in the driveway, dressed in Mr. Barry's black, fifty-year-old tuxedo and my father's pants, ready to leave to pick up my date but sweating it out in the still-hot evening sun. My father had just returned from taking the car to the store, something he never did but that he did that evening, and on the way there he heard sloshing under the driver's seat. Now he pulled from under the seat a bottle of Yellowstone, the high-proof, low-price whiskey I'd bought earlier that day at a bootlegger's and prematurely concealed in the car.

He looked at the whiskey, at me, at the whiskey. He made a noise of deep contempt. "Stay here," he ordered, and disappeared into his woodworking shop. He returned with a paper bag. He uncapped my cheap whiskey and poured it out on the drive, then handed me the paper bag. Inside was a fifth of Antique, the bourbon made at the distillery where he worked. "I don't want to *ever* see a son of P. D. Johnson drinking cheap-ass whiskey," he said. He stalked off.

For Larry's sixteenth birthday Fred and Kathy bought him a car. With it came freedom and popularity—it was still a time, even in California, when a car-owning teenager was not the norm. Larry was pressed into service as errand boy and chauffeur for an increasing number of friends.

When time came to choose a college, he applied to and was accepted at schools near and far away. He chose to attend the Claremont Colleges because they were far enough to put some distance between him and his parents, but near enough that he could accomplish a spontaneous visit.

He came to maturity at the height of the Vietnam War. He grew hair to his shoulders, one thick mass of wavy ringlets—in photographs he looks like Little Lord Fauntleroy gone hip. He fought with his parents over politics, but on the most significant issue parents and son were united: Under no circumstance would he go off to war. Fred hired the best attorney he could find to secure and protect Larry's draft deferment. After college Larry went to graduate school at Michigan, partly by way of pursuing his interest in teaching, partly to obtain a student deferment, and partly to leave California, in search for the first time of his adult wings.

My family lived under the largest and longest of the knobs, Muldraugh's Hill, a forested limestone outcrop that stretches in a green, hundred-mile arc around central Kentucky's Bluegrass. Behind it lay Fort Knox, headquarters less for gold—by the 1960s most of the gold had left for New York, or Europe—than for the United States Army armored divisions, whose commanders liked Muldraugh's Hill and the Kentucky knobs because the terrain was vaguely similar to Vietnam.

On summer nights we adjourned after supper to our backyard to watch their practice wars, reflected from clouds brilliant as sunset until long after sunset, flaming red and orange from the bombs and tracer flares and tank maneuvers at Fort Knox. Then my oldest brother joined the air force and went off to some secret Southeast Asian assignment, and we moved inside to watch the *CBS Evening News*. First the war in Vietnam, then the war at home: demonstrations and riots, in Watts and Harlem, then Detroit, then Louisville, growing always closer, or so it seemed to the white men of my town. With all those men my father loaded a pistol and kept it handy, ready to defend his family from the enemy beyond Muldraugh's Hill.

He kept an anxious eye turned outward, while his family split from within. Television brought us images both of the war's ugliness and its unpopularity, at home and abroad. My brothers and I watched and made our choices: two of us to the military; a third married and with a sole-support deferment; me, the youngest, a draft resister.

My older brothers gone, my father and I were left at home to watch Walter Cronkite alone. We spoke rarely and then in sarcasms, in arguments posed and left hanging, delivered as if to the room at large but directed at each other. We found and flayed each other's weaknesses with the intuition and accuracy of lovers; we were, after all, father and son. "Goddamn hippies," my father growled, watching footage of rock-throwing rioters. "Ought to shoot every last one." The image shifted to wind-tossed palms silhouetted against flames towering from napalmed villages. "Our tax dollars at work," I muttered. For a brief moment the violence at Kent State gouged open our festering quarrel and I addressed him directly. "What if one of us happened to be crossing that campus and was shot?" I cried. "Only what you deserved," he said. "Ought to have stayed at home."

As the war in Vietnam expanded, so did the width and depth of the gap between us. Only the women of the family, my mother and sisters, preserved an uneasy truce, a delicate exercise in Southern manners, where the art lay in saying as much as possible about anything, nothing, so long as it wasn't Vietnam, or race.

One spring day in my senior year I arrived home from school to find my father home from work early, surrounded by his friends, a fifth of bourbon open, its cap in the trash. Seagram, my father's employer, had awarded me a scholarship, paying all expenses at any college in America. "Where're you going with all that money?" somebody asked, and I knew the answer. In 1971, in rural America west of the Appalachians, there was only one answer. I was California bound, to see in living color the world I had known in black and white; heading for a place as far from and as different from the family and the old country as any American place could be.

My father's friends and the parish priest warned against letting me go. "He'll come back a hippie," they said, taking care that I was in earshot. To my father, California was a place like any place, a word like any word, a part of this nation because the news told him it was so. All he knew of this distant, palmy place was what he had seen on television and surely that worried him. But he was a man of honor, who believed that I had earned this choice. He did not stand in my way.

After graduating from high school I left Kentucky three months early, going in June to participate in the National Debate Tournament, held coincidentally at Stanford, where I'd enrolled for the following autumn. The day before I left, a high school friend took me out to drive around and drink, and after two beers she said, "Watch out for the soup."

"The soup?"

"They put drugs in your soup," she said. "I saw it on Walter Cronkite," and probably she had.

Speaking on labor relations, I lost out in the tournament's first round, the judge noting for my benefit that *steel* was pronounced with one syllable, *oil* with two. That fall at Stanford, much to my surprise and disillusionment, my classmates mocked my country accent and ways. After all, I told myself, as children my classmates and I had participated in the same mass culture: the same Walt Disney, the same *Lucy Show,* the same *CBS Evening News.* I counted myself as one of them—I rebelled, grew my hair, narrowed my vowels, burned my bridges—only to find that they did not share my sense of our fellowship. Instead they saw me as I was, a Southern country boy, no matter how long I grew my hair, no matter how I protested. "But I'm *not* from the South. I'm from Kentucky!" I'd say. "We went with the North!"

"North of what?" they'd ask, puzzled. They knew about the Civil War, of course, but they couldn't believe I meant *that* war, half a continent distant and more than a century past. Only now, after years in San Francisco, can I hear how funny I must have sounded to these children of prosperous suburbia.

The Christmas after my freshman year in college I returned to Kentucky with shoulder-length hair and the announcement that I was registering as a conscientious objector. At that first supper, in front of family and guests, my father called me a fool, a solid, old-fashioned word that cut deep. I stood and left the table, a violation of sacred manners and a gesture whose defiance and contempt I knew he understood. An hour later we both sat ourselves in front of Walter Cronkite, each determined to demonstrate to the other that nothing had changed, neither of us conceding by so much as a word that the gap between us had become an open breach. We sat and watched and forged a brittle silence in the crucible of the wood-grain box.

In the following summer I was called before my rural county's draft board. I told my mother I was going on a date, asked if I might borrow the car, asked her to cut my hair. I secretly arranged for two high school teachers to accompany me as witnesses. After two hours of cross-examination the board, most of whom were acquaintances of my father's, granted me a conscientious objector deferment. I told my mother the news via telephone. "Good," she said. No one mentioned the war again. The subject disappeared into the vast conversational graveyard that mannered cultures reserve for sensitive subjects.

Thirteen years passed, in which my father and I spoke about little of greater significance than the weather, until the day when I drove him to the doctor's office, for what would be the last of his chemotherapy treatments. For more than a year after his surgery for cancer, my mother had driven him to these appointments, but now he was too near death and she could no longer bear to be in the presence of the inevitable.

In the doctor's office: My father sat in silence, intimidated by the magnitude of what he faced and by walls covered with diplomas from distant schools (Holy Cross, Columbia, Michigan). I picked up a year-old magazine and pretended to read. The doctor, a Yankee transplant to this rural place, bustled in late. Filled with self-importance and chatter, he had my father's sleeve half rolled up and was about to inject the first hypodermic when my father raised his hand, stopping the doctor in midsentence. My father gestured across the room, to where I was hiding behind the magazine pages. "This is Fenton, my youngest son. A Stanford man."

I drove him home from the doctor's office that day, through an autumn rain. Sugar maples and dogwood and staghorn sumac flamed against limestone cliffs, scarlet leaves and bone-white rock brightened by the wet, as water brightens seashells. On that last drive, my father directed me to the long way home: down the side roads and lanes of his childhood, along the river, across one-lane, oak-planked, cable-and-girder bridges, past deer camps, past the distillery (closed) where he had worked, past the foundation of what had once been the peeling clapboard house where his children had been born, and whose shingle-roofed, brick-walled, indoor-plumbed replacement he had worked for and built. "I married your mother here," he said, pointing out a small brick country church. I nodded and kept driving. "I shot my first deer here," he said as we descended a stony ridge. I kept driving. I felt his groping to say more. I offered him no encouragement.

We touched the tender edges of our thirteen-year-old wound, cut into our lives by the war in Vietnam and by television, enlarged by our own stubbornness and pride. We touched and drew back— the nearness of his death could not change this. Still, I was at his side, driving him for the last time through the landscape of his life, the only countryside he'd known, which he'd given to me and which I'd left to go west. In that almost-wordless hour we acknowledged our blood ties, stronger than politics, stronger than television; stronger, in their way, than my departure for California. Long after his death, I am torn between remorse, that this moment was so short, and gratefulness, that it happened at all.

Larry and I were children of two different, great historical moments. He was a son of the traumatic dislocations of twentieth-century Europe. I was a son of the great migration from the farms to the cities that in those same years emptied the American countryside.

We were both sons of cultures that placed high value on those who came before, but Larry bore the greater burden. I carried my family's elaborate genealogy with me, but the Nazis had poisoned his family's memories, to leave in their place a history whose simple recollection constituted an act of courage.

In each of our cultures—his European and Jewish, mine Southern and Catholic—the burden of blood and history and manners rode heavy and hard. Then we found ourselves in California, where history is only as old as the latest tract development and manners are limited to a newspaper column read mostly for laughs. Maybe this provided the deepest resonance between an only child born of emigrants and the youngest son of a vast, thoroughly American family. We were attracted to each other by our superficial differences, then bound by a mutual understanding of the depth and layerings and resonances of our complex, stratified cultures, each laden with traditions of hospitality, friendship, and ritual. Matzo balls or hush puppies—in the end the recipe doesn't much matter. What matters is the presence on the table of those doughy, bland balls, the living presence of the shaping hand of history.

In a small German town early in this century, a train packed with soldiers of Kaiser Wilhelm's army pulls from the station, while from the crowded platform Larry's grandmother and his peach-fuzzed father toss bags of sandwiches into their outstretched hands. A half a world distant my teenaged father dashes downstairs to toss water-soaked blankets over a moonshine still, burning out of control in the basement of my family's tavern. An instant passes, and thirty years—now Nazis are searching the house next door to where Larry's parents are hiding. Stuffed under the floorboards, Larry's father calls out an offering to St. Anthony if he is not discovered; while in the New World my parents flirt at a roadside tavern in the Kentucky hills, where they dance to the big-band tunes of Paul and His Privates. Twenty more years and I am sitting in the high-ceilinged, poplar-planked classroom where I pass the long months of my seventh grade, autumn into winter into spring, writing and rewriting my name under the unblinking eye of God; while on the glamorous side of the continent Larry thrusts his autograph book at Lucille Ball's mother, who elevates him into the company of the elect. On a winter night in Kentucky, Brother Fintan brings his companion into my life. On an autumn afternoon in Paris, Larry signs a credit card imprint as he checks into the American Hospital.

All these stories telescope into the present, this moment in which I am among the survivors, not at all a self-made man but a walking convention of these stories and countless more in one particular ongoing intersection of space and light and time, in which I understand what is gone and not gone; what I have lost (two loves, father and friend), what I have gained; how the dead live on in us, their lives now our lives, their stories living on and acted out in our own.

IV

From the time we resumed dating, Larry pressed me to meet his parents. He telephoned them for conversations, which seldom lasted more than a few minutes but which were a regular feature of his daily routine. "You call your parents *every day?*" I asked, early in our knowing each other.

"Well, *almost* every day."

I held my tongue, though privately I considered it another way his parents were holding him back from leaving the nest.

More than once he interrupted his calls to them to hand me the phone. "Say hello to my mother," he'd said once.

"But I don't know your mother," I hissed. "What can you say to someone you don't know and have never met?"

"Nothing, anything. It doesn't matter." Larry shook the phone at me.

"I'm still in my underwear," I said. "I refuse to talk to your mother when I'm wearing nothing but underwear." I bolted from the room.

One day he cornered me in the kitchen, phone in hand. "Just say hello. For me."

I took the phone from Larry as if accepting a snake—I understood what this meant: the first step toward becoming a son-in-law. Kathy and I spoke in the briefest and most formulaic of conversations.

"She was no happier about that than I was," I said after Larry hung up.

"Oh, you're imagining things. She's delighted that after all these years I have a boyfriend."

It had been eight years since Larry's last serious relationship. In the interim he'd dated, sometimes seriously, but his parents had grown accustomed to having him to themselves.

That Christmas I agreed to drive south with him to spend a night and a day at his parents' house. From there we would drive to visit my sisters and nieces, who lived in San Diego. I suggested that while in Los Angeles we stay at an empty apartment my brother-in-law kept for when he was in town on business. "No need to do that," Larry said. "I'll take care of everything."

Early on the morning of our departure Larry phoned his mother. I pressed him to skip the call. "You'll be seeing them in ten hours," I said. "They know you're coming. Surely you can skip this one day."

He rolled his eyes. "The good son," he said, and dialed. Later that morning we were caught in rush hour, and though his ten-minute conversation could hardly have made that much difference, I fumed over the delay.

Once on the freeway I held out an olive branch. "I admire your parents for letting us stay at their house together. My mother's great, but if we went to Kentucky, we'd probably end up in separate rooms."

Larry fiddled with the tape deck—he was searching for tapes of French radio he'd recorded on his last visit to Paris. He shoved in a cassette—Radio NRJ, France's leading pop station. A sultry-voiced chanteuse swung into a Madonna imitation. "Well, they don't really know that you're spending the night."

I turned full sideways to look at him. "You're not telling me you haven't told them about my coming along."

"Hey, don't get so upset. It'll be okay. I promise."

A tractor-trailer let out a blast from its air horn. I jerked the car back into its lane. "Larry. Maybe you could tell me what you have in mind?"

Silence.

I took his hand off my leg and laid it on his own. "I'm not showing up as your uninvited, unannounced boyfriend who happens to be in need of a place to crash for the night. I wouldn't do that even if we weren't lovers. You can drop me in Oakland before I'll do that."

"Okay, okay, I'll call them again."

I stopped at a pay phone just off the Bay Bridge. He talked for five, ten, fifteen minutes. I sat drumming my fingers on the steering wheel and considering, more seriously than at any point in our knowing each other, calling the whole thing off—not just the trip but the relationship itself. I could figure only one explanation for why he would put us in such an awkward situation—that by springing me on his parents he hoped to bypass or overwhelm their objections to my presence in his life. This was a scene and a role that I had no interest in playing out.

He returned to the car looking grim. "It'll be okay. Once I talk to my mother in person, it'll be fine."

"Larry, we can stay at my brother-in-law's apartment."

"I made a reservation at a hotel, if it comes to that."

"A hotel," I groaned. "We could have stayed with no trouble, and for free, at my brother-in-law's place."

"I'll pay for it. Of course I'll pay for it."

"I'm not letting you pay for it. If we're going to stay at a hotel, we're sharing the cost."

For the seven-hour drive I adopted a determined cheerfulness, but as we descended from the Tehachapis into the Los Angeles basin, I grew first tense, then resigned. I would trust in manners—mine and theirs—to avoid bloodshed. I would think of myself as an actor onstage, a last-minute understudy called to act in an unfamiliar play, where I asked nothing of myself beyond that I get through without muffing my lines.

At his parents' house, one of those modest seaside bungalows built by the thousands in Los Angeles immediately after the war: Kathy was tiny—less than five feet tall and matchstick thin; Fred was stocky but short. Larry was their brawny child, evidence of the benefits of vitamin-enriched bread and California sunshine.

Still, he was a comfortable height for the bungalow's doll's-house scale. Whereas at six feet–plus I came close to brushing the door lintels. Around every corner, on every shelf, I encountered in-law hazards—delicate porcelain figurines, the only things Kathy and Fred had salvaged of their life in Europe, lying in wait for my careless step or thoughtlessly thrown-about hand.

Kathy had prepared a welcome-home feast: matzos floating in chicken soup, Wiener schnitzel with spaetzle, sauerkraut, potatoes, beer, and a thick, rich chocolate cake for dessert. We sat to dinner—I squeezed into the dining table nook, smacking my head on the chandelier. Kathy said something in German. "*Muti!*" Larry growled.

We took up our tableware. I was acutely conscious of my hands—how big they were! "Ask Fenton about his work with the *New York Times,*" Larry said to Fred, who obliged. I plunged into a description of the life of an occasional feature journalist. Kathy interrupted, handing a dish of potatoes to Fred and asking him a question in German.

"Speak English, *Muti!*" Larry turned to Fred. "Ask Fenton about his teaching."

Fred gamely took up the subject. "Your teaching," he said gravely.

I set about describing the creative writing program where I taught. Kathy interrupted with another question directed at Fred.

"*Muti!*" Larry implored. "Speak English!"

And so on into the evening. With each course I felt myself growing taller and bigger and more awkward. I was relieved when Fred suggested he and I adjourn to the living room, leaving the dishes to Larry and Kathy.

Dressed with impeccable care, Fred carried himself with an elegant reserve. He was handsomely proportioned in the way of many small men—barrel-chested and with broad shoulders, though he shuffled as he walked, partly from age, partly from his chronic back pain. He was almost ninety years old when I first met him, but his silver hair curled thickly over his forehead. A gentleman of an older, European school, he wore a dark suit for that first, informal supper at home.

Like father, like son: He and Larry shared the same full, seductive lower lip, the same flawless smile, the same thick and wavy hair. Both had strong foreheads and deep-set blue eyes; both loved bad jokes.

For an hour and more Fred told stories of Larry's childhood— the time Larry got lost at a Dodgers game; the time his son criticized his high school German teacher's accent. Then Fred came to a pause, leaving me groping for something to say. I knew so little of Fred's life, and what little I knew seemed sensitive. But Larry showed no sign of returning from the rear rooms, so I awkwardly asked Fred to speak about the war years.

His face closed, not severely but with certainty. "This we may talk about at some other time." I understood that the subject was off-limits, at least for an outsider.

I looked at my watch and stood. I excused myself and walked tentatively down the hall, to meet a flustered Larry emerging from the back room. "I can't spend the night with you," he said. "She won't allow it."

I pondered this a moment. Larry spread his hands. "A Jewish mother," he said. "The perfect son." In the end I found myself staying at a nearby hotel.

Alone in that room, I considered the enormous burdens of love, its two-edged sword, how large and daunting the responsibility of knowing when to cling and when to let go. My parents released me, last of their children, into the world to make my own way— financial necessity, if nothing else, dictated that route. Whereas for Fred and Kathy, Larry represented more than "just" a child—he speculated to me that they chose his name exactly because it sounded so American. Later I would learn that though Fred stayed in touch with his first wife and his daughters, their relationship was strained, another of the casualties wars wreak among their survivors; psychological injuries that are seldom tallied but whose impact on culture and history is as great or greater than that of the numbered dead.

Fred and Kathy wanted their only child to be American; more than anything, they wanted to claim this nation as their own. Larry would grow up speaking English as his native tongue, excelling in American schools, attending American baseball games. He would marry an American girl and have American children. He was their surety, proof that they had left behind the Holocaust.

And he completed their family unit in a way particular to only children. Every storyteller learns early on the triangle's remarkable combination of strength and complexity, in which pairs form bonds that are then complicated by the presence of the third party. I began that evening to perceive, however dimly, the grandness of the stories into which I had intruded, how they'd intersected to build a unit tighter even than that of my isolated, sprawling family; how Larry's bonds had been forged from and by history itself.

I thought about this: how whole and unconditional his parents' love, what a wonderful thing it was, even as I saw its weight, how it held Larry down, how he was caught between it and finding and being himself; how any partner of either sex whom he might introduce to the family would find himself or herself disturbing a delicate equilibrium. I thought of this family's history, how intricate and complicated and filled with darknesses and sunlight my imagination could barely envision. Any child would want to relieve his parents of such a burden by taking it on himself; but at what cost?

After Larry's death and not long before his own, Fred read a short, early draft of one of these chapters. He offered compliments; then, as I was rising to leave, he said, "We were not as good as you make us to be." He refused to elaborate.

Of course, I thought then, I think now. I am recounting what I have been told, and what I have been told is what Fred permits himself to remember.

We forget the memories that hinder our continuing on; we cherish and embellish those that give us hope. From our stories we each compose our private opera, for playing and replaying to ourselves and others. This is memory's triumph—it filters and shapes the past into a package suitable for remembering. And this is memory's tragedy: All that shaping and filtering is finally so much stage play, for history exacts its dues independent of what memory wants. As I fell asleep, I thought of Larry, his parents, their histories. *Nothing is ever lost*, I thought. *Nothing is ever escaped.*

V

How we came to love, how we found each other:

Growing up, I had accepted this as the way things were and would always be: I had no capacity either to give passionate love or to receive it. I had so deeply and profoundly accepted this given that I had no awareness of my own self-contempt. As a teenager I thought passionate love between men was both psychologically and physiologically impossible. Murder, rape, thievery, lies—these were ugly words for ugly acts, but words existed to name them, they took place within the realm of what could be spoken about. I had never heard words to describe the desires that of their own accord visited me. A man loving a man—I had never read of this or seen images of it; I had never experienced it in any way other than in the recesses of my own desire, a place so ugly (I assumed) it was beyond the pale of words. To defend myself against my desire I constructed an elaborate wall around my heart, so high no one could see in and I could not see out. How might I be expected to know what lay on the other side?

In college I alternated between binges of studying and binges of drinking and smoking pot, both ways of escaping who I was. Then I graduated and moved to Washington, D.C., to take a job as a press secretary for a U.S. congressman. Here I heard reports of places where men met men. The newspapers covered the murder of a prominent man at a memorial near a military base, where he had gone to seek some kind of love. I changed my bicycle commute so as to bike past that place, slowing each time to survey the scene and to wonder if some day or night I might be courageous or desperate enough to stop. At nights I walked city streets—I'd heard of blocks where men met men, but I didn't know which blocks or how I would identify such men or how I might approach one or what I would do if I were approached. I walked the streets aimlessly, then arrived home late. Loveless and (I believed) incapable of love, I went to bed, to be awakened in the middle of the night by thoughts of suicide. I rose and wrote cheerful letters to distant family and friends.

Then I was twenty-two years old, and I found for the first time in my short life that strangers were smiling at me. I wondered why until I figured out that I had been smiling at them. In my Capitol Hill office my boss asked, "What's got into you?" My coworker shrugged. "Oh, you can't ask much from *him*. He's in love." I turned away to hide a blush of pleasure, guilt, shame (*How can she know? What's giving me away?*). But her speaking gave me permission to name to myself what was happening: love.

I'd met him, and his girlfriend, at a Valentine's party given by a mutual friend. For four months I had arisen at dawn each Saturday and Sunday to bike fourteen miles across the busy city to reach his house. I spent the day with him and rode back. He came to visit me in his car (a souped-up, cherry red GTO in need of a new muffler—I heard that muffler's growl two blocks distant and my heart executed an involuntary backflip). After he left, I lectured myself: *I'm in control. We're just friends.*

Then he began to visit my dreams.

Too many of these dreams and I biked fourteen miles to his house, then invited him to go on a bike ride. I rode as far as we could go and farther to exhaust myself and him, and when I had ridden past exhaustion I found I was still driven by the energy of love and I sat him down and said, "There's something I have to tell you. Something you ought to know."

I looked out at the greening trees of June—I was too frightened and ashamed to look him in the eye, but my heart was in my mouth and it spoke words that filled me with shame: "I love you."

"And I love you," he said.

I was choking with shame and fear that I would never see him again, but love was stronger than shame or fear and so I made myself repeat words I thought I would never say to any living being. "You don't understand. I *really* love you."

He took my hand. "And I *really* love you."

This is what I remember: The ache in my calves. The clear hot blues and greens of June. The damp warmth of his hand in mine.

Some months later I was living with this man, in a small apartment in a large city where I knew very few people, none of them allowed to acknowledge that he and I were lovers. The love that I had denied for so long blossomed in this garden apartment into which daylight never shone, but it was confined there as surely as a tropical orchid to a hothouse—one step out the door and I concentrated on hiding my joy in my discovery that I was capable of love, that I was in love.

I had heard about love this overwhelming—I had read about it, seen it melodramatized in countless advertisements and movies, known some people to whom it had happened. I knew about this love: It happened between men and women, and when it happened, they got married. Or maybe they didn't, but either way, it happened to men and women, not to men and men.

I had known women: friends, sisters, a girlfriend or two. My mother. With each of them I had been in control. I had felt at various times anger, affection, impatience, the whole range and panoply of emotions, but nothing from which I couldn't walk away to some other place, where I could be alone until once again I was thoughtful, reasonable, in control.

Now I was with a man, and he and I were fighting over some impossibly trivial matter—whole milk or low-fat? The argument escalated. He was still seeing his girlfriend, a woman whom he'd known for years. She knew me but did not know about me, that I slept six of seven nights with her boyfriend.

This, of course, was what we were really fighting about, but I was afraid to understand this and especially afraid of what I'd have to make of it if I did. On that seventh night I slept alone in a large bed in a small apartment, to be overcome by emotions too vast and suffocating to comprehend. For all my short life I had defended myself against my self. Now I was losing.

My lover assured me, "You are most important to me. You are first in my heart." I knew he spoke the truth, that he, too, could not see his way out. To tell his girlfriend the truth was at once too obvious and too terrifying. If he gave her up for me, if I demanded the obvious and he complied, it would mean that the two of us really were in love, that we were both in the place that for a year and more we had pretended was not there, and that until now I'd not allowed myself to believe might exist. Love had led me into another country, into the foreign territories that lay outside the wall around my heart, and I was terrified of losing my way back.

What I didn't understand: There was no way back.

The argument escalated until I was seized by a rage so vast that all I could imagine was hitting out at this man I loved. The insatiable hunger of my fury was the measure of my love—I had never wanted to commit violence in this way because I had never loved enough that it mattered. My balled fist held inside it my love and a great deal more, years of denial and desire and hiding. My fist opened and closed of its own volition until it stayed closed. I knew that if I stayed here, my fist would act out its will.

I ran from the apartment and walked the streets and imagined this: A long, sharp knife in my right hand. My heart in my left hand, round and red with life, and as it beat in my hand I took the knife and cut out of it all that had to do with love.

I walked the streets until I was sure my lover had left for his job. A few weeks later I moved to the farther side of the continent.

What is the cost of cutting love from the heart? I have spent a good deal of time considering that question, and this is part of what I have learned: The cost translates into acts that can be counted and tallied and for which we all finally pay. Violence against others, violence against oneself; bigotry, drug addictions, suicides, assaults, murders, or the simple, dull passing of a life given to self-pity, self-denial, and bitterness; contempt for others, so as to reduce them to something like the contempt one feels for oneself.

Whereas Kathy disliked returning to Germany, Fred returned every year beginning in 1954 to Bad Wiessee, a spa in the German Alps where he'd regularly stayed in the 1920s and early 1930s. He drove a German car, read the *Frankfurter Zeitung,* owned a German dog—a testimony to the depth and persistence of his cultural imprint. Across those summers at Bad Wiessee he reclaimed his language, which is to say his culture.

Each summer Larry joined him there for a week or two, partly by way of a vacation, mostly so that Fred could show off his handsome, bilingual son among the dwindling circle of friends and business associates (for the obvious reason, mostly gentiles) from the days prior to the war. Larry and Fred took short walks or sat on the veranda; mostly they talked, seldom about matters of the heart, often about Larry's career choices and ways he might make better use of his facility with languages.

His encounters with love were variations on themes so familiar to gay men. In college he became infatuated with a classmate who was uncertain about his sexual identity. Larry fell prey to the guilt-ridden and hopeless longing that so many gay men must work their way through. After college he had sporadic affairs with women, but he had no enjoyable sex until New Year's Eve of his second year in graduate school at Ann Arbor. That night he was picked up by a man whose lover was out of town, and though he made clear to Larry his situation, no newcomer to the laws of desire can ever believe they are so inflexible.

Larry was disappointed again, but in the great tradition of gay men he became friends with both his one-night stand and his partner, and he came to find great comfort from knowing them. For the first time in his life—he was now almost thirty—he knew men who referred to each other as lovers, who had formed a stable household complete with a dog and a cat, who had gotten about the business of building a life.

Eventually Larry dropped out of graduate school and returned to California, to San Francisco. He took care to locate himself close enough to visit his parents easily but far enough away to maintain some emotional distance.

Not long after moving, Larry met a man with whom he promptly fell in love, with the fervor and some slight desperation of one come so late to romance. His boyfriend was starting a small business, a pizza delivery service in Bolinas, a treacherous twenty-mile drive up the coast from San Francisco. If they were to have a relationship, Larry would need a car; very well, he would buy a car.

He consulted his father, who in turn consulted his friends, who pronounced that a Volkswagen Rabbit was the right car for a man in Larry's situation. At some point his new boyfriend remarked casually that a stick shift would get better mileage and require less maintenance than an automatic transmission. Armed with this research, Larry marched to the local Volkswagen dealership and bought a scarlet, manual-transmission Rabbit, though he'd never driven a stick shift in his life.

I imagine him picking the car up at the dealership; maybe he made a deal with his salesman—in exchange for a driving lesson, Larry would buy the car. I see him chugging home, encountering for the first time the mysteries of a manual transmission on San Francisco's crowded, steep hills. In the Rabbit's slow, jerky progress up Market Street, I see both Larry's hopeless lack of motor coordination and his absolute faith in the power of love to accomplish anything, up to and including changing gears without depressing the clutch. And who am I to be a skeptic? After all, he must have made his way home.

I left my first lover determined to give heterosexuality a last chance. I would go straight, I decided; I would return to where I'd gone to college, to the suburbs of San Francisco, a choice of destinations that speaks volumes about the vastness of my ignorance, or maybe the wisdom of my intuition.

I was surely, woefully naïve, but I had inherited my parents' Depression-era pragmatism. After some short while and no small amount of agonizing, I understood the impossibility of forcing myself to be what I was not. I undertook the labor of accepting myself as I was.

On New Year's Day, 1978, I moved from the suburbs to the city proper, to share an apartment with Miguel, the friend of a friend, one of the few openly gay men whom I knew. It was another step toward learning to accept and love myself. And it was San Francisco in the late 1970s, those innocent and exhilarating years when it first seemed possible for gay men and lesbians to live and love openly.

Miguel had been born in small-town Texas, son of a Chicana mother and a father he never knew. As a child he'd been abused, sexually and physically; at sixteen he got himself to California by selling his body in bus station bathrooms. Through some superhuman strength and with the help of government loans, he completed the course work (though, typical of Miguel, never the thesis) for a master's degree in classics from the University of California. He was fantastically beautiful, with anthracite hair and dark eyes and the high cheekbones of some long-dead Zapotec chief. Far more than I, he was a child of the late twentieth century: dislocated, conversant in multiple cultures but belonging to none, an outcast who found in San Francisco's incipient gay community the first place he might call home.

As I returned to my new apartment that New Year's Day, Miguel called from his bedroom. Would I mind giving him a hand? Drawn by the prospect of camaraderie and by the companionable odor of pot, I walked the length of our flat.

I nodded at Miguel's friend, sitting cross-legged on the bed, transfixed (so I thought) by the music: Christa Ludwig working her way through Carmen's completely corny, absolutely thrilling flirtation with the handsome, love-struck Don José. Against one wall a spray of scarlet gladiolas doubled itself in silver and black mirror tiles.

This is what I thought, a country boy on my first evening living in the city: *Gladiolas are tacky*.

A layer of marijuana haze hung at eye level. My roommate sat in an armchair, arms extended, an elastic strip knotted around one biceps.

I admired his bulging veins. He held up a hypodermic. "Crystal meth. Try some?"

"Oh, no thanks." I tried to sound as if I were declining a stick of gum.

"After it hits, I'll be out of it for a while." With the needle he pointed at a bottle of isopropyl alcohol, some cotton swabs. If I would be so kind. Ease the needle from his arm. Swab the puncture wound.

Of course. No problem.

He held the hypodermic to the ceiling, tapped an air bubble to its top, gently squeezed the plunger until a droplet squirted from the needle's tip. Then he laid the needle against the flat of his arm, that smooth bole of brown flesh. He inserted the needle into a vein, shut his eyes, and pushed in the plunger.

> Yes, there we'll dance the seguidilla,
> While drinking our fill of Manzanilla,
> Close by the ramparts of Seville,
> At the house of my friend Lillas Pastia.

Christa Ludwig sang that blood-stirring habanera while I pulled the needle from Miguel's arm.

He was lost in some interior place where things were speeding by faster and slower than in my own world, where he was in charge, where fate was his servant, where the events of his life came to him rather than the other way around. In the bright bead of blood that quivered on Miguel's skin, I received my first understanding of the place I had come to. I swabbed his arm with rubbing alcohol.

I became an observer of the accelerating gay life of the late 1970s. On Saturday evenings I arrived home just as Miguel was heading out on the town. On Sundays I rose to meet him at the home of a mutual friend, where fifty or so of the men they'd met the night before arrived for a Sunday-morning party in the backyard hot tub. I was drawn to this careless, hedonistic, no-holds-barred celebration of sexual freedom, but always I wanted to write, and all those parties, all those clothes, all those drugs, took time and cost money, and as a struggling writer I had little of either.

In my second year in San Francisco, I applied to graduate schools and was accepted—one nearby, one in the Midwest. "The Midwest?" Miguel was incredulous. "A gay man would leave San Francisco for the Midwest?" I saw his logic. I wrote the Midwestern school and declined their offer of placement and financial aid. I would stay in San Francisco, I decided, though I would find another place to live—I was growing wiser, I was getting city-smart, I was figuring out what the fast life entailed and how much speedier it was than I.

While I was still searching for another place, Miguel found a new roommate, a painfully young man. He'd just been discharged from the navy because he was gay, a nice instance of discrimination that at the time we accepted as simply the way life worked and would always work.

I sensed immediately the new roommate's instability and the unhealthiness of his treatment at the hands of Miguel, who alternated between lavishing affection on him and treating him with contempt, leaving him (on one occasion literally) out in the cold. I warned Miguel against treating him so inconsiderately. Miguel dismissed me with a wave of his hand: "You're just being paranoid."

None of my business, I thought, and in any case I'd be moving soon.

A night or two later, a friend handed me a symphony ticket he wasn't using. The program that night: Mozart, Ravel, Steve Reich, Bach—masters in using repetition to musical effect. Afterward in the lobby I encountered by chance a man I'd been dating, and I invited him back to my place.

The next morning I offered to take him to brunch. On our way out of the apartment I greeted Miguel's new roommate casually. Did he know where Miguel was? "Out on the town," he said.

The apartment was a typical San Francisco railroad flat, long and skinny, with rooms opening one by one from a central hallway. When my date and I returned from brunch, we entered and walked down that hall, to have each room reveal a new scene of destruction: Every window broken. The kitchen floor inches deep in the shards of an eight-serving set of stoneware. The toilet ripped from the wall, its porcelain tank shattered. The bathroom walls hammered to bits, the tub overflowing with broken plaster and tile. The sink wrenched from the wall (the strength of his rage!), its pipes spouting water. The walls spray-painted with four-letter imprecations against Miguel, against the navy, against the new roommate himself, against his family. Miguel's bedclothes torn to shreds, his closet emptied, the clothes ripped in pieces. The trash cans set afire. In Miguel's room the new roommate sat cross-legged in the middle of the floor, with Christa Ludwig's *Carmen* (the only album he'd left unbroken) on the stereo. He was trying to slit his wrists.

I spent the day checking him into the psychiatric ward at the Veterans Administration Hospital. When I arrived home that evening, Miguel was sitting calmly on the slashed couch. He held out an open palm with a pill in the middle. "Have a Valium," he said. I sat on the floor and wept.

Seven A.M. the next day: The graduate program from the Midwestern university called, offering me a last chance to change my mind. I thought about city life, and my time trying to fit myself into it. "What the hell," I said. "Why not take a break from the city." And so I came to spend the early years of the 1980s—years when HIV was establishing itself among San Francisco's gay men— more or less removed from the disease, in a small college town in the Midwest.

Coming out to my mother: We sat on the deck of the wildly impractical cabin my father had built in the woods not far from where I grew up. He had been dead for two years; I was about to publish my first story with a gay, somewhat autobiographical character. It had won a major award and was to appear in a big-city newspaper, and I understood enough of the workings of fate to know that concealing its publication from my mother was an open invitation to circumstance to drop it in her hands.

I told her I was gay—I opened my mouth and spoke the word, looking into the trees, looking anywhere but at her.

"I kind of suspicioned as much," she said—my mother, who when speaking in the presence of her children had always taken such care with her grammar. In that moment I felt our relationship transform itself from parent/child to that of peers. In that moment I acquired a sexual and romantic life. At thirty-two years old I became an adult.

I told her how I'd struggled to be the man others wanted me to be. I could probably have a relationship with a woman, I said, but that would just be drawing my partner into what would surely be a lifelong struggle. "Besides," I said, "I'd be spending so much time and energy trying to be the person other people want me to be, when I already know who I am. I could be giving that effort over to getting about living my life—"

She interrupted, speaking with vehemence. "You have to get about living your life," she said. "That's what's most important."

Larry stayed with his first partner for two years; they lived together for a year and a half, during which they adopted Willy, Larry's cat. After his partner's pizza business folded, Larry and he formed a sight-seeing company specializing in tours for foreigners—while his partner drove the bus, Larry conducted the tour in German or French. The bus broke down once too often, the company failed, the relationship dissolved, a victim partly of Larry's lover's slowness to love, partly smothered by the enormity of Larry's need.

After some floundering Larry obtained his teacher's certification and began work at Berkeley High. His parents continued to send him money—it gave them pleasure to see him enjoy their gifts while they were alive. But their financial support added to the burden he carried as the bearer of his parents' love and expectations.

In describing those days, Larry characterized himself as possessive, sometimes petulant—"I loved like a child," he told me once. His first relationship fell prey to the strains of the early 1980s, when San Francisco dangled in front of gay men that smorgasbord of apparently endless sexual temptation.

After their breakup Larry dated around—he dated a lot, judging by his address book and our occasional conversations on the subject. He fell in lust with a psychiatrist—I was touched to find among his notes evidence of the same, ordinary preoccupation with status and money that dogged me at that memorial service where Larry and I had met. "Cute, and nice, and *a psychiatrist!*" Larry wrote breathlessly. But the psychiatrist was not long at Larry's side; he was shortly to meet and fall in love with Miguel, my first gay roommate.

Seven years later, Larry and I met at Miguel's memorial service.

That I should live far from San Francisco during those years when it was most risky for a sexually active gay man to be there—this was a matter of chance, but it was not chance that Larry invoked when he so often called himself lucky, nor was it chance that I was invoking on that evening, shortly before he died, when I applied the word to myself. When he said—when he taught me to say—that we were lucky, we did not mean that chance had favored us—clearly it hadn't, in visiting Larry with HIV. The luck of which we spoke was something larger and more profound.

We were lucky in the many obvious, conventional senses of the word, of course. Larry was spared the terrible, two- and three-year dying that we'd both witnessed among friends. I was spared watching him endure that death. We had loving, supportive families and friends. We were prosperous enough not to be overwhelmed by the financial burden of dying. Larry had insurance. I was and remain HIV-negative.

But Larry, a smart man, called himself lucky before he knew how he would die. He brought me to describe myself that way, even as I knew that few of our contemporaries could understand how we might say that. How could we come to call ourselves lucky—he who was infected and would die, I who was not but who would lose the love of my life?

VI

A few months after my first, Christmastime visit with Larry's parents, I sat in a windowless cubicle in San Francisco's District Health Center #1. A pleasant, solemn aide snapped the elastic tourniquet from my arm. Usually I look away when having blood drawn, but I watched this blood fill the vial dark purple: the color of my life and in it, or maybe not, the uninvited guests, the invisible party crashers. I had not told Larry I was taking this, my first HIV test, because I knew that in the two weeks it took to get results he'd worry more than I.

As I watched the vial fill, men emerged from my past to visit this present moment, Fenton at the District Health Center. There weren't many of those men, really, for me, a nice Catholic boy who excepting a few ill-considered moments had reserved the intimacy of penetrative sex for partners with whom I shared some kind of love—partners who, as luck would have it, had all tested negative. But those all-too-human moments with those few, other men, before anyone suspected the existence of HIV: The Mexican, brutally insistent until I, young and dumb, let him have his way. The salesman so eager to fall in love, and so convincingly infatuated (he wasn't a salesman for nothing), how could I say no? The suicidal graphic artist, nothing but danger here, but too beautiful for me to resist.

With each of these men I'd had unsafe sex only once, but once is enough and in life as in law ignorance is no excuse. I was old enough to know this truth, young enough not to believe it: that a life may be destroyed by a single unconscious act, committed unaware of its implications; that history shapes itself on the couch or in the kitchen as surely as in the war zone or the legislature.

Two weeks passed. The day I was to receive my results I phoned Larry early. "Let's get together for supper," I said. I tried to sound casual—surely he could hear my forced casualness? "I've got a meeting in your neighborhood."

"What meeting?"

"Oh, too long a story to go into now. I'll tell you this evening."

The hour of my appointment: Streets were clogged, I was delayed. The only parking place within blocks was too small. Parallel parking, I bumped the car behind me, setting off its alarm. My hands trembled. If I'd had a brick, I'd have heaved it into that bleating block of metal and glass.

My particular messenger from the fates was a cheerful blonde, a displaced Hungarian who was puzzled when I showed little joy at the news that I'd tested negative. When I told her my boyfriend was positive, she gave me a look I decided to ignore.

On the short walk to Larry's apartment I considered how to tell him that I had been spared when he had not. I thought of the range of human response to such news: not what he *ought* to feel, but what he surely *would* feel—envy, anger, bitterness at the unfairness of fate.

At his apartment, at the supper table: I took a deep breath. I wanted to blurt the news out in one sentence, to say *test* and *negative* in the same breath. "So I took the test," I said. My voice broke; I lost my breath. His eyes widened in alarm. "I'm negative."

His joy brought him to his feet. He clutched me in his arms, dancing me around the room. Lost in his embrace I wondered, *What could it mean, that someone deep in misfortune could feel such joy at another's good luck?*

The best theory for the naming of California:

In 1508 the Spanish pulp writer Ordóñez de Montalvo published *Las sergas de Esplandiàn,* a picaresque novel whose hero sails not east but west from Asia to reach the New World. In it Montalvo writes:

> Know, then, that, on the right hand of the Indies, there is an island called California, very close to the side of the Terrestrial Paradise, and it was peopled by black women, without any man among them, for they lived in the fashion of Amazons. They were of strong and hardy bodies, of ardent courage and great force. Their island was the strongest in all the world, with its steep cliffs and rocky shores. Their arms were all of gold, and so was the harness of the wild beasts which they tamed and rode.

The Califian women keep a few men not for pleasure—they're skilled in the lesbian arts—but for breeding. Ordóñez de Montalvo dreams of such employment, in this golden land named for its queen, Califia.

The first Spanish explorers of the West knew Montalvo's novel, and its uncannily accurate depiction of the land unfolding before their horses. Their journals and dispatches give no report of Califia and her Amazons, but I like to think she and her tribe lived a few years into the Spanish era. Maybe they encountered Father Serra on his burro before succumbing to smallpox and the despair that accompanies genocide. Can we really know Father Serra never confronted their dark, bare breasts simply because he doesn't mention them in his diaries? Women have never fared well among historians.

That spring I left the place I'd been house-sitting to move an hour or so south to Montalvo, the summer villa of turn-of-the-century San Francisco mayor and U.S. senator James Phelan. Named after the Spanish novelist, Montalvo offers residencies for artists completing works-in-progress. I was to be a colonial for two months while I worked on my second novel.

On weekends Larry visited, and we hiked together into the hills behind the villa. At one point we came to a small creek, across which someone had placed a branch—not as an aid for getting to the other side (the creek was too small and shallow to need that) but to help in keeping shoes dry. I stepped on the branch and was across in a moment. Larry hung back. "What's the problem?" I asked.

"I don't want to cross."

"Why not?" I threw a dismissive wave at the creek bed. The crossing was so simple, second nature to me. For a moment I wondered, *Was he afraid?* Then I dismissed the thought. *Afraid of what? The worst fate would be a wet shoe, and that only if the hiker was clumsy.*

"I'm afraid. What if I fall?"

"So you'll get wet. Maybe. And I'll take you home and dry you off." I returned to the creek bed and held out my hand. "Here. Security."

Larry crept forward—he might be trying to cross Niagara on a tightrope. Rather than taking the crossing in one easy bound, he teetered on the log; but I gave him a tug, and he was on the other side. I was on the verge of a comment on his timidity when I saw the shine in his eyes, his pride at this act of bravado. I held my tongue, but some part of me drew back again at this evidence of the gap between his sheltered suburban childhood and my rural, rough-and-tumble upbringing.

"Mr. Johnson is one of America's finest and most celebrated young authors," Larry announced to his high school class. Sitting behind him, blocked by his desk from the view of his class, I kicked his leg, but he continued the hyperbole. As reading, he'd assigned his students a chapter of my first novel, which had been published in a literary journal and which he'd photocopied for the class.

I'd barely set foot in a high school since my own graduation from a county high school as different from Berkeley High as Kentucky from California. In my school, being caught in the halls between bells was grounds for suspension, a punishment considered only slightly less significant than the electric chair. At Berkeley High the classrooms opened directly to a large outside courtyard, which in turn opened to city streets; drug dealing, gang fights, and violence against teachers were not uncommon. Some of Larry's students sported button-down collars, others wore lip and nose rings, some wore both. In this chaotic environment Larry set out to teach my work— a chapter involving clandestine lovemaking between a man and a woman, set amid the strip mines of eastern Kentucky.

Once before I'd spoken to a high school English class, that time at my high school alma mater. There the students' questions were halting and wondering, centered more around me than my work: How was it possible to live in a really big city, to have these things as part of one's daily landscape—skyscrapers, oceans, traffic jams, palm trees? It was hard for them to imagine such a world, harder still to imagine themselves having a place in it. At Berkeley High the students assumed their own necessity and importance. They spoke of themselves as planning careers, a word I never once heard mentioned in Kentucky. Some aspired to be writers or artists or politicians—they'd been born to prosperity; power, or at least access to it, they considered their birthright.

For the first half of class I moved to the rear of the room, where I accordioned myself into a desk (had I been that much smaller in high school?). Usually we interact with our lovers as part of a dance in which we're one of the partners; here I was watching Larry as if he were onstage.

He was all over the room, but as an intellectual, not a physical, presence. He wore shirts woven from materials (linen, lightweight wool) whose loose drape flattered his build, but he moved with the awkward, endearing gracelessness of a man come late to an appreciation of his body. At the same time his mind was constantly at work, suggesting, asking, pushing, arguing; the classroom equivalent of a gymnast's exercise. "You told me you want to be a writer," he said to one student. "Ask Mr. Johnson about that." He stopped at another's desk. "Don't you have something you've been working on? Maybe Mr. Johnson would take a look at it."

One of his students had been slipping mash notes into Larry's faculty mailbox, and though the notes were anonymous Larry was certain of their source. Late in the class Larry stood behind me and nodded to one corner. "The girl in the baggy yellow pants," he whispered. I glanced in her direction—a Hindi transplanted to America, with glistening black hair and a smooth, dark complexion.

At the end of class he invited anyone who wished to stay after to speak with me. The dark-complected girl strode up. "So I notice the hero in your story has blue eyes," she said to me. "Like Mr. Rose."

"*Protagonist,*" Larry interjected. "That's more accurate than *hero.* For one thing the protagonist might be a woman, and *hero* is a masculine noun. For another, the main character is always the protagonist, but he might not have the qualities we associate with heroes. He might be a jerk."

"Right." She kept her eyes on me.

"In fact the male protagonist in this story is something of a jerk," I said. "Unlike Mr. Rose."

"Mr. Rose has *fabulous* blue eyes," she said.

"I wrote this chapter a long time before I met Mr. Rose," I said, but she was already edging away to join a group of friends.

"They probably dared her to say that," Larry said. "You think she's implying something about you and me?"

"Oh, she's just in love," I said. "And with good reason."

My Montalvo studio faced a formal garden whose wisteria-delirious courtyard was rented out on weekends for weddings. On Friday afternoons the string quartets arrived, set up, and practiced; each Saturday morning I was awakened by their music. Three times every Saturday and Sunday a string quartet of dubious expertise sawed away against a backdrop of platters of tiramisu and the overpowering scent of wisteria. Six weddings each weekend, forty-eight weddings in all, and at each and every one Pachelbel's "Canon."

This was the obvious question, the question implicit in my HIV-test counselor's doubting look, which I asked myself again and again, even as others asked it of me: How could I fall in love with someone whom I knew to have a terminal, transmissible disease? At what point did I commit myself to this journey, closing that door behind me (or allowing it to fall shut—either choice amounts to the same; not to choose, as we so famously know, is to choose)?

Sleeping with Larry at Montalvo, I found myself in this dream:

I am with a friend whom in my waking life I know to be HIV-negative. The two of us are running from other men, living mummies wrapped in bandages and winding cloths. Where their bandages have fallen away, their flesh is bloodied and rotting. They are coming to make us one of them. My friend and I run until we are cornered in a cave, we are warding off our pursuers with our arms . . .

I awoke in terror, to the scent of wisteria growing outside the window, to the chattery song of the western meadowlarks that had arrived with spring, to the mournful groan of a flat cello warming up to the first, tired bars of Pachelbel's "Canon."

I turned to Larry—the force of my bolting awake had awakened him. "Can I tell you my greatest fear?" I asked.

He nodded, after a moment's hesitation—he knew what I was about to say; the unspoken, the unspeakable, that had haunted us both since our first lovemaking.

I lay back, staring at the ceiling—I could barely bring myself to speak. "My greatest fear is that you will die and leave me infected and alone."

In the face of this there was nothing to say, and so he said nothing. For a long while we lay quiet in each other's arms, and in that place I began to understand this: One measure of love is the ability to speak aloud the unspeakable, secure in the knowledge of the bedrock on which you rest. To speak with such frankness of the terrors of the heart—to talk so openly of the demons within, with no fear on either side of rejection—honesty of this completeness is the privilege of true lovers. In opening my mouth to speak, in his hearing me out, I was beginning to understand the nature of a love so whole that in the end it encompassed everything about ourselves, including his disease and our fear of contagion. I was beginning to understand how I might love through pain and ugliness, for better or for worse, up to and beyond death. I was beginning to understand how love offers some kind of victory, the thing that enables us to become larger than ourselves, larger than death.

VII

The first evening I made Larry corn bread, he proposed.

I was making supper in my apartment at Villa Montalvo, banging pots and pans around its tiny kitchen, looking for my cornbread pan, which had disappeared into the maw of some storage box. Larry pulled a square, blue granite pan from under the counter. "What's wrong with this?"

"For good corn bread you have to use cast iron. It holds heat better than anything else. Honest-to-God corn bread only comes in two forms. The heart-shaped muffins give you a soft center. The long pones—the kind that look like little ears of corn?—they give you a crunchy bite all the way through, because the batter gets heated faster in a long, thin mold."

"Like this?" He pulled out my baked-black corn-bread pan.

I took it from him, rinsed it off, greased it, and stuck it in the oven. I explained preheating the pan before pouring the batter, so as to make a crisp crust. I explained the difference between Southern corn bread with its hearty bite, and the soft, sicky-sweet cubes of cake that pass for corn bread in California restaurants.

I pulled out ingredients. "Stone-ground cornmeal. Not the dried-out stuff you buy in a box."

He looked over my shoulder. "All that trouble and you're using margarine?"

"Well, sure. You don't want to have a heart attack, do you?"

"Give me butter or give me death," he said.

I made a great clashing and clattering of pans and spoons and batter to fill the silence that followed.

"That's a joke," he said.

When I poured the batter, it hissed when it hit the preheated molds. I stood back and admired the effect—golden batter sputtering against the black cast-iron pans. "Now, that's a pretty sight."

"So let's move in together. After you leave your artist residency. It's the perfect time to do it."

I gathered the holey socks that passed for pot holders and shifted the pans back into the oven. "I don't think I'm ready for that."

We argued for the time it took the corn bread to bake—twenty-three minutes. I gave him one logical reason after another: We hadn't known each other long enough. We were doing fine living apart. I could never live with someone so messy. I didn't mention, he didn't ask after what I knew to be the heart of the matter. Moving in with Larry represented not just a commitment to the relationship, but a commitment to taking care of him through whatever awaited.

The timer went off. "No," I said. "Not yet. Not now." I pulled the bread from the oven.

"So go with me to France. You speak French."

"I haven't spoken a word of French since I was an undergraduate, when I was a student in Tours. Ten years ago. Fifteen years ago. Besides, I'm going to be in Kentucky this summer." For a long while I'd planned to spend a summer with my mother, both for pleasure and to help her with a long list of home-maintenance projects that had accumulated since my father's death.

"You can fly to France from Kentucky. Once you're there, you pick the language back up right away."

"You pick it back up if you ever learned it in the first place. I spent most of my time in Tours avoiding any situation where I might be forced to speak a word."

"You can listen to tapes. You can borrow my books and review."

The next day he gave me *Langue et Langage,* the same French textbook I'd used in college, and a stack of language tapes. I was driving back and forth from Montalvo to his place once or twice each week—a good hour's drive, and I had nothing better to stick in the tape deck. *What the hell,* I thought.

I listened to the tapes: unintelligible, and they expected me to respond. A sultry woman's voice asked complicated questions in complex tenses ("How would your life have changed if, when growing up, you had lived in a foreign land?"). Then she gave me no more time to respond than if we'd been—well, in conversation. "Hopeless," I told Larry. But I kept listening. It made me feel chic and smart, driving down the freeway listening to French I didn't understand.

A week or so and he raised the subject again. "So you'll come to France?"

"I can't afford to come to France."

"I'll pay your way."

"You will not pay my way."

"Why shouldn't I pay your way? I want you to come. It would give me pleasure to have you there."

"I won't let you pay my way, that's why. You're living in San Francisco on a high school teacher's salary. I won't let you spend that kind of money on me."

Larry shrugged. "I'll manage the money," he said, though when I asked how, he grew vague.

We wrangled across that spring. All the while I kept *Langue et Langage* on the dining table, where I peered into it over breakfast and lunch, staining its pages with guacamole and pea soup. Larry saw it dozens of times and never mentioned it once, even as he quietly went about making reservations.

In the end we compromised. I would buy a plane ticket, round-trip from Louisville to Paris. He would cover most of our expenses in France itself. In return, he would visit my family and me in Kentucky sometime later in the summer—a visit I found myself agreeing to without being able to trace exactly where and when he'd raised the subject.

In mid-June I flew to Kentucky for that long-planned summer visit. I took the French tapes and book along. Weekends I stayed with my mother; during the week I worked on a novel at the rustic cottage my parents had built on a wooded reservoir an hour's drive to the west.

This is what faced me, for eighteen years a city dweller, as I drove a rented car from the Louisville airport to the small Kentucky town where I'd grown up: a summer with my widowed mother, who was living alone in a house that once supported her and my father, along with four daughters, four sons, three dogs (one for petting, two for hunting), a flock of Rhode Island Reds, a half-acre garden, and three hundred quail that my father brought home from the Rolling Fork Fish & Game Club as an experiment in reestablishing the birds (hunted nearly to extinction) in neighboring fields. For two months before leaving San Francisco I had turned down jobs, weaseled out of appointments, left phone calls unreturned. On my kitchen table I kept a running list of things to do during my three-month visit:

1. replace water heater
2. put on new roof
3. tear out wood-burning stove
4. buy air conditioner (window unit)
5. fix leaky toilet

Youngest son, self-employed, I was the likely candidate for these jobs—and for broaching other, more delicate matters:

6. what about money?
7. living alone? why not a dog?
8. love life?

So I arrived at the house to find my mother sharing the porch swing with a new man (*a new man?*), a longtime friend of the family, an eighty-two-year-old Southern gentleman ten years her senior. "You don't think he's too old for you?" I whispered while he was inside. "How much longer—" I struggled for some delicate way to say it. "He's a great guy," I finished lamely. "It's just that he might not be around for too long."

She shrugged. "He's alive, which gives him an advantage over most men around here." When he returned, he put his arm around her, she cuddled up to him. My mother, whom my father hadn't publicly kissed in forty-seven years of marriage!

That Saturday he took my mother and me to the theater (my father had hardly attended a play in his life). Late that night we drove home—the kids (them) in back, the chauffeur (me) up front. At his house I parked in the drive. I waited a few seconds—a thick and delicious moment. Then I cleared my throat. "I think I'll get my sunglasses out of the trunk," I said.

More than anything, my mother wanted someone to take her fishing, or at least to accompany her while she went, but her elderly companion was not a fisherman. A few weeks later I searched out the bamboo poles from the depths of the woodshed. We spent an hour sanding rust from the old hooks. "Every time we fished, Father would make us sand clean every one," she said. "He'd never let us throw away a single hook."

We stashed the bank poles in the trunk and drove to the river, where everything was feeding on whatever was in reach: dragonflies eating mosquitoes, bass and crappie eating dragonflies, catfish feeding on the bottom. A great blue heron stalked the mussel beds. I waded into the water, to be startled by a branch that fell from overhead, plop! It swam away in sinuous curves.

Mother cocked her head, listening. " 'Can't catch when the locusts grind' was what Father always said," she said. But we did. When we returned the next morning, a single pole bobbed and dipped—a nice seven-pound, steel-blue channel cat.

Back home she laid it out on the big stone that had once served as a step for travelers dismounting horses. "So smack it against the rock," she said.

I studied the hot blue sky.

She picked up a hatchet. "This will be tough, but I just can't bring myself to bang 'em against the rock." She raised the hatchet overhead and brought it down—crack!—on the cat's thick, flat skull. She twisted the hatchet from its head, then pulled the hook from its mouth. She considered the rusting hook for a long moment. Then she tossed it in the garbage.

Should I dwell on her strength—plunging the hatchet into the channel cat's steel-gray head? Or on her need—red-faced and angry at the arrival of duplicate billings and threatening notices from her doctor, her hospital, her insurance company, Medicare? I know what we wanted to hear, I and my scattered brothers and sisters: She's doing fine, she loves our visits but doesn't need our help, she has her bridge club, bowling, golf, reading, volunteer work, the church, friends. Over long-distance lines and in letters she has told us this and we believe her.

But a summer is a long time to keep up an illusion. One Monday after I'd been gone for the weekend she dropped her guard. "It's Sunday afternoons that get to you," she said. "There's nobody to call, nothing on television, a million things you can't bring yourself to do. Sometimes I just get in the car and drive." Then she stood abruptly and disappeared, to reappear a half hour later waving a wrench. "I fixed the toilet," she said. I checked it out: The leak was gone.

I was in Kentucky for only three months, but things move fast in California—out of sight, out of mind. To listen to my friends, I might have been leaving for Beulah land. Three months in *Kentucky?* Drop a line, my San Francisco friends said. Let us know how it goes. I could have cut the skepticism in their voices with my mother's hatchet.

That's what struck me over the summer, as I typed away in the basement, the only cool place in the house: How many of my San Francisco friends told me of their parents in the same situation—the nuclear family exploded, its children scattered over hundreds or thousands of miles. *The child is father to the man,* I thought, though more often to the woman. All my friends, some now parents, had parents, most often widows, most often living alone and at some distance from their offspring; some comfortable, most depending in some measure—financial, emotional—on their children.

About that air conditioner and my list of projects. My mother refused to let me buy an air-conditioning unit until they went on sale, which they never did in that long, hot summer. The weekend we planned to put on a new roof it rained. That same weekend we were supposed to take out the wood-burning stove. We *did* replace the water heater. Mostly we went on walks. One moment I was the teacher, the next I was the student. I talked about life in the big city; she taught me the names of birds and plants, and the stories that went with them.

M y father designed and built a summer cabin, then called it the HERMITage, a name he etched on a plank and hung above the door. I spent days writing on the deck. In that hot, dry summer the birds of the field (redwing blackbirds, meadowlarks) took refuge in the deep woods; their calls kept me company until late in the evening, when the whippoorwill's tireless calling and an occasional owl hoot replaced their melodious chatter. At night the silence was a living thing, so large and thick it hurt to hear—the crunch of my biting a carrot echoed like a breaking branch.

I'd brought along a photograph of Larry, bare-chested on a hike we'd taken, and I thought of him in the evenings after my work and reading were done. I recalled a party, shortly before my leaving San Francisco, in which I realized I'd been proud to show him off among my friends. Then I heard the voice of my most particular demon—"There's someone else who's richer, prettier, more successful; there's someone whom *other* people see as higher in the pecking order."

I wasn't pleased by such thoughts, but for my summertime reading I'd undertaken George Eliot and Jane Austen, both of whom deal, often with sly humor, with the pressure on women to "trade up." "A poor girl from the country, with only her wit and a fast-fading beauty to sustain her, must watch out to marry well," or so I could imagine Austen writing of one of her characters.

Larry and I had spoken bluntly of these matters; he was unfazed. He accepted me as I was, this was clear—an acceptance that was seductive exactly because it was unqualified. He had learned this acceptance partly from his parents, who understood the price and the reward of living in and for the moment; he'd learned it partly as a result of his HIV status. Could I love so generously in return? Some large part of my reluctance grew from my character (cool and airy). But some grew from my young man's assumption that my time to love and be loved was infinite—why not drag my feet? I loved with an innocence born of my presumption of immortality, which I'd yet to have seriously challenged. "To move in with you would represent more than a commitment to love," I wrote to Larry.

It would be a decision that the time had come to wrestle with my greatest demons. Such battles are never won or lost, they continue across years, with the person closest at hand most likely to suffer.

It would be trivial to say that I know that love can conquer this. It hasn't, for me anyway, in the past. I do love you, of this I'm sure. Looking back, I'm afraid I've given that short shrift. My reservation begins with my fear that where your love might succeed, mine will fail you, as I have failed others before.

I'm looking forward, very much, to meeting up with you in France, and to having you here in Kentucky in August.

In the middle of that summer, I undertook my first journey to France in fifteen years. I arrived from Kentucky bleary-eyed and culture-shocked, to see Larry pacing the terminal corridor the other side of the customs officers. Once I'd cleared customs, he swept me up in an impassioned hug.

I spent that day napping at the apartment of his friends, who lived in the northern suburbs of Paris. That evening we went into Paris, to sit in a café across from the Tour St.-Jacques and drink glass after glass of wine. For a while I tried vainly to follow the animated French of Larry and his friends, until finally I only pretended to listen while I took in the scene—the endless flow of traffic across the Pont au Change, the brilliantly floodlit Tour St.-Jacques, the music of the language that rose and fell around me, the scent of the cologne that Larry's friends wore. As we stood to go, I turned to Larry to ask in English, "That cologne? Is it what I think it is?"

Larry nodded. "I first started using it here. Vetiver."

"But you're not wearing it now."

Larry rolled his eyes. "I was wondering how long you'd take to notice."

On that first visit, my French was abysmal. With Larry at hand as prompter/translator, I improved exponentially, but each day I caused Larry's French friends to dissolve in laughter for reasons I never understood. At any point requiring even the simplest negotiations, I stood back and let Larry take charge.

During these visits I came to appreciate the value of deliberately inverting the patterns of our relationships. In California, I was the workaholic, running all over town, with a calendar filled with social and business appointments; while Larry's life was consumed by teaching's mercilessly fixed schedule and endless piles of papers to grade. In France, I was the innocent abroad, and Larry was my guide. He made reservations, chose restaurants, charmed the waiter into seating us by the window, enlightened me to the vagaries of the suburban rail system. I was a visitor in his land, and he woke each day to the joy of showing it off.

One day we got lost walking in the vast caverns of Les Halles, lost amid the boutiques, searching for an entrance to the Châtelet metro station. Larry stopped a stranger to ask directions. They chatted for a moment; she volunteered the name of a pleasant neighborhood restaurant. "*Vous parlez français très bien,*" she said to him. "*Comme un français.*" ("You speak French very well—like a Frenchman.")

We walked on. "I admire you for that," I said.

"For what?"

"Going up to a stranger, asking directions, starting a conversation. I can't imagine being that confident in another language. Any language, but especially French. They're so intimidating."

"Oh, their bark is worse than their bite," he said.

When I pass a church, I stop to light a memorial candle. The habit is partly a remnant of Catholic grade school, partly a gift from a culture that valued remembering its past and the names of its dead. Memento mori, remember the dead—a pleasant task; the leaving of a bit of light and beauty in these vast, cool spaces for the next person to contemplate. "I light them for my father," I told Larry as I searched my pockets for francs to pay for the tapers. "And for our friends who have died. It's all superstition, of course, but it's cheap enough as superstition goes."

Toward the end of my stay in France we ate in Le Petit Prince, a late-night Left Bank restaurant. I wanted to order fish, but I prefer red wines to white. I had by now seen Larry question the waiter often enough to give it a try myself. "Could you recommend a light red wine that might be appropriate with fish?" I asked in French.

A look of consternation crossed my waiter's face. "*Non, monsieur. C'est pas fait.*" ("This is not done.")

"I understand. One does not usually drink red wine with fish. But perhaps a *lighter* red wine."

He pointed to the whites.

Had I misunderstood? Was my waiter being especially surly? I looked at Larry's friend. He buried himself behind his menu. I looked at Larry. He shrugged. "Something white," I said helplessly. I was at table in France, after all, and France was proving larger than I.

Facing a menu, I assumed that I might order what I wished, when I wished. This is the heart of what it means to be American: the assumption that the individual triumphs over all; that no social code is more important than the servicing of one's particular wants, no matter how idiosyncratic. Whereas Frenchness is epitomized at table, where every course and gesture pays homage to the terms of the social contract, the precedence of history over the present moment, the preference for tradition over striking out. Americans think each situation must be approached with freshness and originality. The French understand that this is an illusion, that nothing exists that hasn't been done before, and often.

I returned to Kentucky from Paris, where later that summer Larry arrived for a visit. The day of his arrival, I met my mother descending the basement stairs, a clutch of clean sheets over one arm. "You two can sleep down here," she said, "down here" meaning a basement room my father had converted into a bedroom. The beds were singles, but it was the most remote room in the house, which, emptied of its flock of children, had other empty bedrooms. I understood the implications of the room assignment—she'd raised me with the language of manners, I had no need for an interpreter: What you do "down here" is up to you, but if you don't mind, keep it quiet.

On Larry's first evening in Kentucky I took him for a drive through my small town and the surrounding countryside. We stopped first at the Catholic cemetery where my great-grandparents and grandparents and father are buried, where at the side of my father's grave a plot waits for my mother, where the family tombstone is already engraved with the names of their children. Larry's family circle had been decimated by the Holocaust; as a childless only child he represented the end of his particular genealogical branch. As we walked through the cemetery, he stopped me at each tombstone. "Who's this?" he asked. "How are they related to you?"

"My grandfather. My great-grandmother on my father's side. My great-uncle on my father's side." And so on.

"Think of all that family," he said. "What's it like, to live with all that history?"

"Look at *your* family. Your parents carry as much weight of history in one generation as mine do in four or five."

"All that history has to go somewhere," he said. "All that energy of grief"—a phrase that echoes to me years later.

"In my case it gets spread out among lots of kids. In your case it all comes down to you. The sole survivor."

We started back to the car, walking among my ancestors' graves. "So which is better?" I asked. "To live with all that history or to leave it behind?"

He stopped at the cemetery gate. "You pay a price to live with it, I know that much. But you get great things in return."

From the cemetery we drove into the knobs, over one-lane gravel roads that led deep into the hills, past crumbling storefronts where once there had been towns, along the mail route my maternal grandfather once drove in his Model A, past abandoned farmhouses where in the nineteenth century my ancestors had tried to scratch a living from the rocky soil. We stopped on a bluff overlooking the small river that winds through these hills, and that has for millions of years performed its patient work of wearing them down.

Late summer: The river placid below, the sunlight diffused

across the valley and golden against the limestone cliffs. Silence. Larry and I had not been together in a month, not since I'd returned from France; a year after our meeting and we still hungered for each other with the heat of first lovers. Above that old river we kissed, then wordlessly drew apart. We were men in love not allowed to love in this place where we were acutely aware of the real physical danger invoked by one man openly expressing love for another. "Tomorrow," I said. "We can do this tomorrow night, at the HERMITage."

Reluctantly he pulled away. "Imagine a world where I might put my arms around my Fenton in public."

I turned to walk back to the car. "I'm not comfortable with that."

"With what? My having my arms around you in public?"

"Well, yeah, that. At least, not here. But what I mean is, your calling me 'my Fenton.' It makes me sound like I'm a possession. Like I belong to you."

He stopped in midpath, waiting until I turned around. "And don't you belong to me?"

"Well, in a manner of speaking," I said. "I don't know. Maybe it's because we're here in Kentucky. I'm just being neurotic."

"You're being neurotic."

"All the same."

He sighed and patted my shoulder. "Okay. How about this: *A* Fenton."

"Huh?"

" 'Imagine a world,' " he said, quoting himself, " 'where I might put my arms around *a* Fenton.' "

We returned in time for a typical Johnson gathering. Small, by the standards of my family—supper for twelve, like thousands of meals my mother had cooked: Deer roast, thawed from meat my brothers had killed, butchered and frozen the previous fall. Mashed potatoes. Biscuits and sorghum molasses. Heavenly hash— a mixture of fruit cocktail, coconut, and miniature marshmallows.

Corn on the cob, grown by a neighbor. Bright yellow and red tomatoes from my mother's garden. Cucumbers and onions pickled in brine. Peach cobbler for dessert. Larry was effusive about the countryside, effusive about the food, effusive about the company. He fell into my family as if he had been born to it, and my family, for whom congeniality triumphs over all other considerations, welcomed him in kind.

The next day it rained, long and hard, almost the first rain of that summer. Larry and I were so eager to leave we sidestepped family farewells. We made the hour-plus drive to my family cabin in a heavy downpour, but we were oblivious to the weather.

At the cabin we parked in the sodden woods. After he finished construction my father had allowed the access road to fall into disrepair, so that to reach the cabin we walked a quarter mile through the forest, then descended a ladder down a sixty-foot cliff. We walked through dripping trees, the pungent moldy beginnings of autumn rising to greet us as we descended.

We dropped our bags. I pulled Larry outside, onto the cabin deck.

One end of the cabin anchors itself on a house-sized limestone boulder, which across millennia has detached itself from the cliff in a slow slide toward the ravine. The cabin front is glass, opening onto a view of the ravine and the forest. A redwood deck projects over the ravine toward the old-growth beech trees that people the facing slope—giants by deciduous standards, nearly a hundred feet tall, supporting in their canopies a community of birds and squirrels and snakes.

Below the deck the creek chattered happily to itself, an endless monologue about the joy of running free after a long, dry summer. The stillness was absolute, except for the occasional drip of water from the ancient, smooth-skinned beeches and the creek's cheerful babble.

He took me in his arms. "I am one lucky boy. Here in the Kentucky woods with my—with *a* Fenton."

Death has its own powerful attraction. We are all drawn to it in some dark way, much as we're drawn home long after *home* has ceased to have any resemblance to the place where we grew up. The densest among us understands this symbiosis between life and death, love and loss; it's not for nothing that we call orgasms, in French and in English, our little deaths.

But there was nothing romantic about living with a man with HIV. It haunted our lives and our lovemaking. Despite our precautions, Larry lived in terror that he would infect me—he loved me too much not to feel this fear. I lived in terror that I would be infected. After the safest lovemaking we wondered, *What if a drop of his semen fell on a scratch I hadn't noticed? What if I had a cold sore in my mouth, or what if "they" (the medical establishment, who had been wrong so many times) were wrong in claiming that the virus was not transmitted through kissing?* When Larry and I first met, the facts of how people transmit HIV had only recently been established and were still widely questioned. Every time we made love we questioned them in some small secret place. Every time we made love I longed for this: the chance to engage, just once, in this act with the two of us alone; the chance to make love as a couple rather than as a ménage à trois, where death was constantly the third party.

In sadness I recall my fear: not that Larry would die before me—this we assumed—but that he would infect me before he died. Surely that self-absorption was nothing unusual, and yet it governed our relationship. It overshadowed and overwhelmed my native generosity. For a year and more it prevented us from entering into the partnership we were capable of and wanted.

And yet: As we grew to love each other more deeply, the possibility of infection ceased to be my greatest terror. That worry was there, but we knew how to protect ourselves against it, we protected ourselves against it, and while I'd be lying if I wrote that the worry never crossed my mind—it crossed my mind a lot—it was not the main source of my fear. The main source of my fear was this: Each time we made love I took from him a little more of his self, and gave in return a little more of my self, binding us together a little more closely. We were becoming married, in fact if not before the law; we were becoming one instead of two. I saw this happening and rejoiced in its happening even as I feared that when he died, the part of me that I'd given to him would die with him. Each time we made love I gave more of myself to him and took more in return and so enlarged my heart, made it bigger and stronger (like any muscle, the heart grows with exercise). But as we grew more a part of each other, I grew more terrified that when he died, he would take some large part of me with him and that I would fall into the hole he left behind, whose bottom (if it existed) I could not yet begin to fathom.

After our stay at the HERMITage Larry and I toured through the mountains of eastern Kentucky. Toward the end of our journey we stopped to eat an early lunch at a small roadside restaurant called the Iron Skillet: whitewashed cinder block, two twin plate-glass windows facing the road, a gravel parking lot large enough to have dark corners where on Friday nights the pickup drivers smoke pot and drink beer and try to feel up the high school cheerleaders. I did my time at the dark edges of such lots, though there was no marijuana then and I spent those evenings worrying over whether machismo required that I put the move on a girl who didn't inter-est me and who obviously wasn't interested.

Inside the Iron Skillet, Larry inspected the menu carefully, then handed it to me. I put it down without looking. "You're not eat-ing?" he asked.

"I know it by heart. Fried catfish. Chicken-fried steak. Fried potatoes. French fries. Fried country ham. Fried chicken."

"You've been here before?"

"In a manner of speaking."

Our waitress sauntered up, a petite, starched-and-bleached blonde with brilliantly lavender eyeshadow and matching chips of glass in her dangling earrings. She looked thirty and was probably eighteen. "You all in town for the Honey Festival?" she asked.

"Honey?" Larry asked.

"Aw, *honey.*" She tapped his thick shoulder with her finger, then stood back and waited.

"Chicken-fried steak," Larry said. "And a diet Coke."

"No, really, guys, it's a festival. The Honey Festival. Today and tomorrow." A note of disbelief crept into her voice. "You ain't heard of it."

We shook our heads. "We're just passing through," Larry said.

Through mascara-lidded eyes she gave him a long study. "Honey, nobody 'just passes through' the Iron Skillet. Where're you all from?"

"California," Larry said.

"*California.* Wow."

"Actually, I'm from Kentucky," I said.

"Well, y'all check it out." She leaned her hip against Larry's shoulder. "I'm off at three, if you're looking for a tour." She took my order and left.

"You'll regret it," I hissed.

"A tour? You really want to come back?"

"No, the chicken-fried steak."

He left a big tip.

On our last evening in Kentucky, Larry, my mother, and I visited my father's grave, where Larry and I helped her prune and clean the arrangements of flowers and evergreens she replenishes there weekly. Afterward we walked with my mother through the nearby fields of the monastery at Gethsemane, where years before she and my father had thrown picnics for the monks who joined us from behind the enclosure walls. In the sweet tolling of vespers I heard those monks' names, a medieval litany: Clement, Marcellus, Christopher, Wilfrid, Fintan, my namesake. They were almost all gone, drawn away by marriage, secular careers, other religious orders, death.

In the fence rows we heard the scratch and scatter of quail—*lots* of quail, descendants of the Rolling Fork Fish & Game Club quail that my father had imported to these hills and that I'd raised and released. A covey exploded under our noses. The summer heat had broken, the paths were lined with fall wildflowers, which, thanks to that summer with my mother, I could name as we walked along: partridge pea, boneset, goldenrod, ironweed. The sun set in a hurry, the light was low and autumnal; all around us was the knowing that this, another summer, was coming to an end.

Somehow this one gesture summed up that summer: my mother's hand, wrinkled and spotted with age, stripping a dried stalk of purple loosestrife for seed to plant in her wildflower garden. She was careful to point out to Larry that she'd scattered some seed on the ground; some for the birds, some for propagation. "Some for whoever might come along next year," she said.

VIII

Larry and I were entwined in an afternoon nap in a quaint coastside hotel in Cancale, a fishing village located in Brittany on the western edge of the Bay of Mont-St.-Michel. To the east the spire of the church of Mont-St.-Michel pierced the horizon. It was a warm, lazy afternoon—we were sleeping off the tension of the drive from Paris with Larry's friends, who drove like—well, Frenchmen (120 mph on the autoroute, 80 mph on the winding, narrow country roads).

Larry and I had taken to reading whole books aloud to each other, and as I woke, he began reading aloud from our latest choice—*Sir Gawain and the Green Knight,* which he'd selected for this trip to France because it's small and portable and because it tells the story of a journey. *Sir Gawain* is a long, immensely entertaining thirteenth-century poem (we were reading a translation into modern English) that recounts the adventures of Sir Gawain of King Arthur's Round Table.

King Arthur's court at Camelot is winding up its New Year's celebrations when a ghastly green guest arrives uninvited, a knight "green and huge of grain . . . garbed all in green . . . the same hue as his horse." The Green Knight tosses this challenge at the assembled Round Table: He will accept one blow from any knight present, on the condition that in exactly one year that knight will seek him out so as to allow him to return the favor.

The assembled knights hem and haw and look at the floor and the ceiling, until young Sir Gawain rises to the challenge. He takes up his ax and in one stroke slices off the Green Knight's head, which rolls this way and that, spewing blood as it's kicked about the floor by the knights and their consorts.

But the Green Knight chases down his decapitated head and

picks it up. Speaking from the Green Knight's hands, the severed head congratulates Gawain on his skill and looks forward to their return engagement a year hence. Head in hand, the Green Knight mounts his green horse and rides from the hall. The knights and ladies look at one another, at Gawain, at one another, at Gawain (you're in *deep* trouble now, man).

The year passes poetically enough, until time comes for Gawain to meet his fate. True to his word, brave Gawain mounts his magnificently caparisoned horse Gringolet.

> Said Gawain, gay of cheer,
> "Whether fate be foul or fair,
> Why falter I or fear?
> What should man do but dare?"

"'What should man do but dare?'" Larry repeated. He poked me in the side, then raised his right hand over his head. "Farm out," he said, a dumb joke he'd picked up from me. "Right arm."

"My turn, idiot." I took the book from him.

Gawain journeys north on Gringolet. After meeting and surmounting many trials he reaches a mysterious castle. There he's welcomed by his host, Bertilak, and ensconced in luxury. Each day Bertilak goes out hunting, leaving Gawain to rest but exacting from him a promise that each will give the other all the gains he comes by during his day's adventures.

While Gawain rests, he's visited by a stunningly beautiful lady. On two succeeding days she tries to seduce him; for two days running he rejects her wily advances. Her seductions failing, she tries to give Gawain gifts. As her guest, she argues, he can't politely refuse—he has a duty to accept. But each day the virtuous Gawain declines:

> Before God, gracious lady, no giving just now!
> Not having anything to offer, I shall accept
>   nothing.

My turn to poke Larry in the side. "My point exactly. I can't afford to give gifts, so I don't want to accept them from you."

Larry took the book from me. "What you're giving me is more valuable than anything I ever thought I'd be lucky enough to receive."

I turned to look out at the shallowing sea. The legendary tides of the Bay of Mont-St.-Michel retreat so far and so fast I could watch them withdraw. Behind me Larry took up reading the story.

As the water in the bay dropped, it gently deposited dories and skiffs and trawlers on vast sand flats, where they sat tilting drunkenly on their keels, awaiting the tides' return. From our third-story window they looked like toy boats on a toy strand in a small toy town on the coast of Brittany, where barely a few centuries earlier knights (maybe green) rode horses (maybe green) through a landscape thickly peopled to this day with mysterious, massive stone monoliths. How had these stones come to be set upright, when they were too huge and heavy to have been raised by the technology of their era?

Behind me Larry's voice rose and fell, its familiar, funny stop and start a symptom, I sometimes thought, of a bilingual person's constant choosing between equally viable but different words.

Magic comes in threes, the most powerful prime number: three persons in God, three wishes in a ring, Cinderella's third night at the ball. At their third and last meeting, the lady tempts Gawain with her most powerful gift: the green girdle that belts her waist. He who possesses it, she says, can come to no harm. Gawain is virtuous as ever, but he's got the Green Knight to worry about, and surely, facing such a threat, the magic girdle wouldn't be a bad thing to have at hand. He yields and accepts the girdle, then hides it immediately.

That evening, Bertilak returns from the hunt and tells of his day, then heaps furs and "fine fat flesh" at Gawain's feet. He asks Gawain what he may have come by during his day. Gawain studies the ceiling. He does not mention the magic girdle.

The next day Gawain rides out wearing the girdle hidden under his armor. Nearby, in a green glade, he meets the Green Knight. True to his pledged word, Gawain kneels, baring his neck for the great blow.

The Green Knight swings and misses once, then twice with his great ax; the third time he nicks Gawain's neck. Gawain springs up, contending that he's fulfilled his side of the bargain. He pulls out his sword, ready for fair fight, to discover that the Green Knight has removed his helmet. He's none other than Bertilak, Gawain's host.

Bertilak lectures Gawain for concealing the girdle—a lie against a friend, however minor and defensible, is a transgression against sacred hospitality. Bertilak tells Gawain that he swung the ax twice and missed to reward his guest for refusing the beautiful lady's advances—she turns out to be not his wife but the witch and temptress Morgan le Fay. Bertilak's nicking Gawain's neck on the third blow was to punish Gawain for his duplicity in hiding the green girdle.

Gawain sets out to return to Camelot, properly chastised.

> Now Gawain goes riding on Gringolet
> In lonely lands, his life saved by grace.

He's welcomed back to Camelot by Guinevere, King Arthur, and the assembled knights, who agree that despite his slip from perfect virtue he has upheld the honor of the Round Table.

"*Hony soit qui mal pence,*" Larry read. "Let shame be on him who here thinks evil." I heard the book fall to the floor. Larry wrapped his thick arms around me in a bear hug. I thought of his illness, the dark, distant, evil cloud in this brilliantly sunny day, the two of us reading in bed in the middle of the afternoon (such luxury) on the magical coast of Brittany. I thought of the Breton countryside with its huge stone pillars mysteriously raised upright, and I thought: *In this strange world of green knights and monoliths, who can say what miracles may be possible?*

IX

After that summer in Kentucky and France, I ended my self-imposed homelessness by moving into a studio apartment in San Francisco. In my first weeks there, I received in the mail a note from a friend, sent posthumously and bearing wildflower seeds, which he'd asked that I scatter in his memory. The creative writing professor at San Francisco State who'd helped me get a job was diagnosed with *Pneumocystis*. And James died, sweet baby James, the smaller-than-a-minute secretary at the office where I'd worked, who wore lavender suspenders and fake leopard-skin pants and called me Mr. Fenton. Shortly after our return, Larry started AZT. Miguel's old lover—Miguel who had been dead for over a year, at whose memorial service I'd met Larry—came to town and looked like walking death.

Thirty-one, twenty-nine, thirty-eight, forty-one years old. They're (I would write *we're*, but I'm no longer sure of my community with these men, a community I spent years learning to take for granted. Even though I'm a gay man, am I *of* these infected men, a part of them? Or—as an HIV-negative man—am I apart from them? Which is of greater significance to our identity—how we love, or how we die?)—these men, my chosen family, are living longer but it's getting to them, it's getting to us. I decided that I could tell who's positive by looking and listening. How often and in what way does he speak of the future? How is he choosing to spend his time and money? In men who were "progressing" (such a stupid word), I saw the skin tighten on the cheekbones, the hair lose its luster.

Could I stand to watch this in someone I was coming to love so deeply? Which would be harder: coming to one's own death? Or watching the death of one's love?

I signed up to take the HIV test for the second time. While awaiting the results I got myself into something of a state—far more so than the first time I took the test. Had I tested positive that first time, I might reasonably have concluded that I'd contracted the virus from one of my possible exposures in the late 1970s. Now, more than a year after meeting Larry, if I tested positive, I would surely have contracted the virus from him, however careful our lovemaking had been.

I tested negative.

That autumn a straight friend of many years visited San Francisco. We arranged to meet at the Café Flore, the city's hangout for the terminally unemployed and that strange breed of writer who's able to work, or at least put up a good show of it, in public settings. When I told my friend that I was contemplating moving in with an HIV-positive man, he grew visibly angry.

"You must have some kind of romantic death wish," he said. "You're nuts."

When I first met this friend, he was in love with a woman who'd lived with her lover for many years. At night my friend stood in the street below their window, crying and calling her name. Once, when by chance he encountered her boyfriend in a restaurant, he decked the guy.

Suppose this, I said to my brilliantly passionate straight friend. Suppose your heart's desire fell in love with you. And then suppose as you're about to plunge into bed, she reveals that she has a good chance of dying in the next four to six years, of a disease that is transmissible through one particular sexual act. Either you have to forgo that act, or you have to take care to protect yourself when engaging in it.

Suppose further, I said, that you know that any other woman you encounter is likely to be in the same situation; that so far as you know at that moment, *you* may be in that same situation. I asked, Do you pack your bags and head for the door? "You might walk away from this café and be hit by a truck tomorrow," I argued. "You might get injured or killed in a car wreck any day, every day. Knowing that, do you forgo a chance for deep, passionate love because your lover may die in a year, or in five or six years?" Protecting yourself against a disease transmitted only through unprotected penetrative sex and needle drugs is not so tough, I said. Which was not to say that there's no risk.

"But life is *about* risk," I said. I quoted Sir Gawain. " 'What should man do but dare?' "

I'd raised my voice, I was growing heated, but no one much noticed at the Flore, where raised voices in general and this conversation in particular were old hat. Had you lived before penicillin, I asked my friend, would you have been celibate because of syphilis? I answered my question: No, you would have chosen your partners carefully and used a condom, as I have. And—the unfortunate but unavoidable truth—before condoms, he and I would most likely have risked all anyway.

"There's no such thing as one hundred percent safe sex," I said. "There never has been. It's just that antibiotics allowed us for a few decades to cure whatever diseases we contracted along the way. And HIV has ended those few decades."

And we're men, I argued. All of a sudden men are at risk for contracting a fatal, sexually transmissible disease, and suddenly everyone notices that sex has the risk of really serious consequences, which can't be addressed with a shot of penicillin. But for women, sex has always had serious consequences.

My straight friend thought a moment about all I'd said. In anger (at my naïveté? at the truth of what I'd said?) he stood and walked away.

All brave words and blustery front, rendered more blustery by my increasing fear at Larry's slowly but irreversibly worsening health. Numbers, just numbers, the good things down, the bad things up, a low-grade fever here and there, but nothing that doesn't happen to us all, or so we told ourselves, whistlers in the dark.

But my need to talk won out over my fear of words, as good a definition of a writer as I know. Larry and I had long, painful conversations that never really ended. I began to push the issue gently. When was he going to tell his parents? What decisions about continuing or discontinuing medical care did he want me to make, in the event he wasn't capable of making them? But we could not yet speak the terrible words, and so we discussed the latest medical advances or exaggerated the good side of the ambiguous news about his health, and we went on falling in love.

Christmas Eve, 1988: I was back in my home county in rural Kentucky, driving my mother's car, my cousin riding shotgun. We were gossiping about the family tree, more sober than most judges, when a drunk driver in a one-ton pickup truck ran a stop sign. Nobly if unintentionally I placed us between him and the telephone pole toward which he was hurtling. He hit us broadside at 60 mph.

The drunk driver emerged from our collision unscathed. I endured for the first time in my life the indignity of being scraped off the pavement, immobilized on a stretcher, and rushed to the county hospital emergency room, sirens screaming. I spent the night getting x-rayed ("Xeroxed," I said later through a haze of Demerol). The next morning a chain-smoking doctor showed me the X rays, pointing out the ribs that had been severed—jagged black space between their ends. Looking them over, I thought back to my conversation at the Café Flore. "Any one of us might be hit by a truck tomorrow," I muttered.

"What's that?"

"How do the ends find their ways back together?"

"You know all that meaty stuff when you eat ribs? That's just muscle, and it'll jam them back together. Or maybe it won't and they'll just heal over separated. You'll feel these for a long, long time."

This I had cause to remember in the next weeks, when any time I turned, coughed, or laughed, my muscles jammed my ribs back together. When this happened in the middle of the night (all quiet, with the tent of the blankets as a reverberation chamber), they made this charming grinding and clicking noise.

Once I was back in San Francisco, Larry seized the opportunity to let his Jewish mothering instincts run wild. He brought me food and books, dealt with mail, stayed over every night. My first novel was in the midst of prepublication labor—copyediting, last-minute changes. Each evening we lay in bed proofreading in the only reliable way—one of us reading aloud the page proofs, while the other followed along with the manuscript. Later that spring when the novel came out, Larry was its most ardent promoter, buying copies at different bookstores until I forbade him to buy more, then turning up weeks later with copies he "chanced to see" while out shopping.

Not long after my Christmas accident Larry began volunteering at the San Francisco AIDS Foundation, at a time when it was making the transition from struggling, marginalized nonprofit to large conduit for funds from many sources to AIDS- and HIV-related projects. Larry's task was to draw up an organizational chart of the multiple federal agencies that dealt with HIV, plotting their lines of responsibility and authority as well as key personnel. The patchwork of agencies was complicated, and Larry spent hours on the phone clarifying agency relationships (or the lack of them), then additional hours mapping out the chart itself. As the project grew more complex, I suggested that he try executing it on his computer—he could more easily draw the chart, with its constantly changing names and layout, with a graphics program than by hand.

I'd made some critical assumptions—among them that I could teach and that Larry could learn a graphics program. We dove in one evening when I'd finished fixing supper for us both and he was at his desk reading over some student papers.

Larry took a pile of composition papers from a chair and moved it to the desk. "Have a seat."

I pointed at the desk. "We're going to need at least enough room for the computer and the printer." We spent the next few minutes shifting more stacks of papers. "What are these?" I asked, holding up a stack of unopened envelopes.

He looked them over. "My father gave me some oil stocks a long time ago for my birthday. Maybe these have to do with them."

"You have stocks and you don't know what's going on with them?"

He shrugged. "If they strike it big, I figure somebody will let me know." He lugged in the computer.

"We're going to need some space to take notes." I pushed aside some cassettes. "Do you want these?"

He looked them over, then let out a whoop. "I've been looking for these for two years! They're tapes I used in a class I taught on French literature."

Two hours later we'd cleared enough space for working. In the process I unearthed an old address book with the names of his past dates. I flipped through it. "I envy you knowing all these people in Europe," I said. "All your old boyfriends, no doubt."

"Oh, they're just people I met here and there. I always tried to get people's addresses in case I was back in their neighborhood on a later trip."

I opened to the first page. "Paul Adrineau."

"Oh, I met him in a bar one night in Nice."

"Etienne Gilliers."

Larry thought for a moment. "With a Paris address? I think he picked me up in the Bois de Boulogne."

"Friedrich Muller."

"A *doctor*," Larry said triumphantly. "I visited him when I had shingles."

"You never told me you'd had shingles."

Larry shrugged. "I didn't see any need to," he said defensively. "It doesn't necessarily mean anything. Anybody who's had chicken pox can get shingles." He snatched the book from my hands, and I let it go. We both knew that shingles can be a warning sign of immune system problems, but I let the subject drop. He was right, after all—shingles wasn't necessarily an indicator of problems to come, and it wasn't as if he'd lied to me about it; he'd just overlooked or forgotten details, in a way that presented his past most favorably for his cause. Still, the omission left me uneasy.

More debris on his desktop: two expired passports, a copy of his birth certificate ("Hey! I've been looking for that for ages!"), a file of his cat's vaccination records, several years of bank statements (most unopened), programs from plays he'd seen years before in London's West End (as we unearthed each playbill he recounted the evening, complete with actor and director names and a critical evaluation of each production). At midnight I'd just begun to decipher the graphics program that came with his computer.

"Maybe you should do it the old-fashioned way," I said.

"Maybe I should do it the old-fashioned way." We went to bed. A month later he drew the chart by hand.

For Larry's fortieth birthday I told him we were to go for a barbecue to an old friend's house. Then I invited all his friends to surprise him.

Early that afternoon I made him a cake, a four-layer chocolate affair. I studied the recipe. I considered my margarine supply, then pushed it to the back of the fridge and went out to buy butter.

I was midway through making the cake when my phone rang—Larry was calling to tell me his cousin was planning her wedding. At first I'd been invited, then I'd been disinvited. The wedding was to be in a relative's apartment. The in-laws would be present but the space was so small they'd prefer Larry to come alone.

He arrived at my apartment just as the cake was coming out of the oven. While I iced the cake (another stick of butter), he engaged in phone skirmishes with his family. He told them he'd refuse to attend the wedding unless he could bring me—an upsetting announcement in a family so small.

Later that afternoon, Larry's birthday surprise accomplished: a friend videotaped the party. At one point Larry explained to the assembled friends the complicated genealogical, cultural, and social negotiations that he'd engaged with his family. They had come around to his point of view; I would be invited. Larry would stay with me at my brother-in-law's Los Angeles apartment.

Watching that videotape of his fortieth birthday party, watching him tell this story, I hear the noisy pride in his voice, and I understand how important this battle was, for him and for me. At forty years old he was asserting himself not against but within his family; asserting his right to passionate love, and so asserting himself as an adult. For how do we define adulthood, except as that place where we begin romantic relationships? In my case, my coming out to my mother had marked the transformation of our relationship from parent/child to that of two peers. Once we could acknowledge what we'd both long known—that is, my sexuality—neither I nor she had to continue pretending that I had no romantic or sexual desires; in a word, that I was still a child.

At the party this moment came—Larry opening my present, which I'd wrapped in last Sunday's comic pages. He tore into the paper, scattering ribbon and scraps in all directions, to pull out (of course) a thick wool sweater, more practical than stylish. "Life as a sweater theme park," I joked. Though it was a warm day in May, he pulled it on and gave me an impromptu kiss.

A few weeks later, at Larry's cousin's wedding, his family asked us to hold up two of the corners of the *chuppa*, the fringed canopy that in a Jewish wedding protects the bride and groom and that represents the stability and peace of the home they're establishing. I was honored to be welcomed. Larry beamed at me from his place at the adjacent corner.

It was the end of the spring of our second year together. Larry was finishing up his semester at Berkeley High, while I worked on an article for a local magazine. I was reading over the last-draft pages while Larry finished grading papers. "You don't need to write lots of comments on them," I said. "It's the end of the semester. They'll just look at the grade and take off for the beach." He nodded and kept writing notes.

At the end of the evening he brought Willy in and sat opposite me at the table, tossing a rolled pipe cleaner for the cat to fetch until I looked up from my work. "So have you thought any more about our moving in together?" he asked.

I answered truthfully. "No."

"Why not?"

I marked my place, laid the pages aside. I held up my hand, counting in the French style I'd learned the previous summer, beginning with my thumb. "One. You're a pig. It's true."

"It's true."

"It would drive me nuts."

"I'd have a separate room that was mine and I'd keep all my stuff in it."

I held up my forefinger. "Two. We get along fine as is. Why rock a good thing?"

"It could be better."

"Three. We're two *very* different people. I'm a country boy at heart, child of Depression survivors who saves every scrap of wrapping paper—don't deny it, you've made fun of me for it. And you're a city boy, child of urban Jews who haven't put their hands in dirt in four centuries. Those kinds of things shape who you are."

"We complement each other."

"Four. Your T-cell count is going down. This is what happens." I made myself say it. It was necessary and important, I thought, for one of us to be realistic about his illness. "It's been going down, and so far as we know, it will keep going down. If"—I could not bring myself to say *when*—"if you get sick, I'll have to take care of you. And I want to take care of you—don't get me wrong. I'll be there for you. But I think it would be better if I were living in a place where I can get away from that. I have to keep my work going somehow. It will help me keep myself together. That would be harder if we were in the same household."

A small silence. I bent over to give him a kiss. "I have to return these galleys by the weekend."

"So let's go back to France. For the bicentennial."

"The bicentennial of what?" I asked, though I was only stalling.

"The French Revolution, *mon petit chou*—1789–1989. *Allons, enfants de la patrie, le jour de gloire est arrivé,*" he sang, throwing his arms grandly about.

We argued. Paris will be packed, I said. We'll never get a flight.

I've already made our plane reservations, he said.

I don't want to impose on your friends, I said.

I've booked us a hotel reservation for a few days surrounding the fourteenth of July, he said. Then we can go to the country. "You said last year you wanted to go into the country."

My back to the wall, I spoke the real issue. "I can't afford to go to France. And I'm not letting you pay my way two years in a row."

"I didn't pay your way last year."

"You paid more than your share." I was adamant. He was too generous, I said. Though he'd never told me as much, I had figured out that his parents largely financed his travels. "It's good that your parents give you money—you're their only child. But I'm uncom-fortable at your turning around and spending that money on me. I'm too independent, I guess. Or just plain ornery." I was not going to be his subsidized lover. No trips to France. That was that, case closed, period.

X

Paris, July 14, 1989: the *bicentenaire de la révolution française*—the French bicentennial.

Larry and I danced at the various street *bals* scattered around the city; we finished up at the *bal gai,* where the gays and their friends danced to disco music pumped over the quays, while overhead floated the serene towers of Notre-Dame. In the graying light of a Paris dawn Larry led me inside the cathedral, where he stopped in front of a prie-dieu and pulled a five-franc coin from his pocket. I looked at him quizzically. "I'm lighting a candle," he said. "In memory of your father."

On our first trip to Paris, Larry had taken me to the *Guide Michelin*'s three-star attractions (*vaut le voyage*—worth the trip). Now we set about looking through the two-star draws (*mérite un détour*—stop by if it's on the way). We both considered the Cimetière Père Lachaise, where Paris buries its notables, *vaut le voyage,* however the tubby Michelin icon might disagree.

"I have this theory," I said as we stood waiting for the metro to the cemetery. "About the French. They only speak French to torture me. As soon as I'm out of earshot, the entire nation heaves a collective sigh of relief and lapses into English, which is what they speak all the time when I'm not around."

"You're just taking it personally," Larry said. "Tell me where we're going."

"Pare Lachaise."

Larry set about tutoring me on the particular challenge of the French *r*. "*Père.* The tongue against the teeth. Exhale as you say it."

"*Pare.*"

"*Non, non, non, mon petit entrepôt*" ("my little warehouse," a nickname he'd coined based on our prodigious consumption of pastries). "English is a lazy language—it all happens in the back of your mouth. To speak French you have to work the front of your mouth. Use those teeth and lips." He demonstrated. "Make faces. If you feel like a fool, you know you're getting it right. *Aa—eee— ooooh—oooo*—and *eu-eu-eu*," that peculiarly French pursed-lipped *eu*. He demonstrated, an exaggerated *p* and an aspirated *r*. "*Père Lachaise.*"

"Pare Lachaise," I said. "Really, this is hopeless."

We ate our lunch at Proust's tomb, a plain flat rectangle of polished granite in the heart of the cemetery, adjacent to the columbarium. Larry had risen early to visit Fauchon, Paris's highest-brow delicatessen (though the word is inadequate to describe this vendor of the food of the gods). Under the full-leafed horse chestnuts, surrounded by the ghosts of the glory of France, we ate *délices de Fauchon* and talked about love.

He wanted a commitment to monogamy. I pointed out that since I'd met him, I'd not been to bed with anyone else in San Francisco.

"You had that one-night stand in New York."

"That was New York. It was a one-night stand. I don't even remember the guy's name," I said, though I did. "I was traveling. I get adventuresome when I travel, it's what travel is about. It has nothing to do with you and everything to do with me. I just like to go out and see how the natives do it."

"You satisfy me so completely I don't even think about looking at anybody else."

"You're in love. Pass the pâté."

He passed the pâté. "And so you're not."

"You know that's not true. I'm in love, all right. It's just that I like to venture out on the town, and one thing leads to another. I don't do that in San Francisco exactly because I know there it's dangerous to our relationship. But what's the big deal about a night with somebody I'll never see again who lives three thousand miles away?" I spread a piece of baguette with pâté and handed it to him. "All it does is remind me how good things are with you."

"Then why do you need to do it?"

"I want to be honest. In fact I'm practically monogamous, you know that. It's just that I don't want to make you a promise I'm not certain I can keep. Because if I give you my word, I'm good for it."

"I know that," he said.

We cleaned up the crumbs of our lunch, then went in search of Oscar Wilde's tomb. "I doubt that the notion of monogamy ever crossed Wilde's mind," I said.

"And look what happened to him."

We took photos of that tomb, its winged demigod defaced by vandals. Larry took four pictures of me, I took one of him: the usual ratio.

We wrangled more over monogamy. Even then I knew that at some level he was right, that my forays in distant cities were not entirely innocent. I was grappling now with my particular demon, my impulse to seek a partner less because he loved me than because he might win some kind of public opinion poll. I was fighting that old demon and most often overcoming it, only then to face this real and terrible and too-understandable quandary: what I wanted was a man who was HIV-negative; what I wanted was an HIV-negative Larry.

Leaning against Wilde's tomb, we arrived at this compromise, half joking, half serious. I couldn't and wouldn't have sex with anyone in the nine-county San Francisco–Oakland–San Jose standard metropolitan statistical area. I would tell him if I had sex with anyone while traveling.

Every relationship comes to these moments, where yes confronts no, where one partner must yield to the other partner's way of being. Larry was domestic by nature; beyond that, he had good reason to want this love to be as intense as possible. He was living, in Flannery O'Connor's memorable phrase, as if he had a gun to his head.

But that is exactly the point, of course. We each live with that gun to our head, however we like to pretend otherwise. To advance into our lives, to open new doors, we have to shut old doors behind us.

I was trying to keep a foot in each of those multiple doors, partly because so long as I had a foot in those doors, I could believe that I was protecting myself; that if Larry died, when he died, I would somehow be unscarred by his death. But this is not how the heart works. The heart knows what it wants and gives itself to what it wants; the head follows behind. My heart was firmly in Larry's hand. In refusing what he wanted, in denying us both this commitment, I kept some doors open, but at the expense of other, more sumptuous rooms. Monogamy, or the lack of it, would not break us up—we were too much in love, both of us, to break up. But after this conversation Larry held a part of himself in reserve, however small, a protected place where he did not allow me to go.

W e took a day trip to Versailles. On our visit the previous summer it had rained, and we'd been confined to the palace interior. This day was lovely, warm and clear. "Let's rent bikes and ride around the gardens," I suggested.

He hung back.

"We'll have a great time," I said. "Great exercise. And the gardens are so huge there's no other way to see them." In my enthusiasm I grabbed his hand and pulled him along.

We rented the only bikes available, balloon-tired clunkers— "girls' bikes," missing the middle stabilizing bar. We tooled around to the far side of the vast cruciform reflecting pool that forms the gardens' heart. I led the way, with Larry wobbling along behind.

On the far side of the gardens we laid the bikes on the grass. "My bike is in better shape than yours," I said. "Why don't we switch?"

"Oh, it's okay. It doesn't make any difference to me. I never learned how to ride a bike anyway."

I stared in disbelief. "You *never* learned how to ride a bike?"

"My mother was afraid I'd have an accident. She'd never let me do anything like that. Then I got old enough that it was too embarrassing to try and so I just didn't get around to it."

"Why didn't you *tell* me? It's much harder to ride these clunky bikes, for one thing. They're so unstable."

He shrugged sheepishly. "You wanted to do it. I figured I could learn from watching you. It was time I learned. I'm doing okay."

"You're doing great." On our return to the palace I hung back, letting him take the lead.

For supper that night I suggested a brasserie across from the Gare du Nord—I wanted to try their oysters, which they shipped directly from the Breton coast. After supper we walked in the Marais, the gayest quarter of Paris. In a shop window I saw a shirt, fashionably black, emblazoned with the French tricolor and motto *Liberté, Egalité, Fraternité*. Such a shirt would play nicely in San Francisco—even I, with my wooden eye for fashion, could see that. "Great shirt," I said.

"I'll buy it for you."

"No way. They won't have my size." I stood next to the window and demonstrated.

"We can check."

"It'll be too expensive."

"It's on sale."

"Look, I really want to get home soon. We have to get up early tomorrow."

We wandered down the street. After a few steps Larry pointed out a patisserie. "Let's get some pastries. We won't have time tomorrow morning to get to a patisserie. You go in and buy them—you need to practice your French without me along."

When I returned, pastries in hand, he was gone. A few minutes later he rounded the corner, carrying a shopping bag. "I hope you bought that for yourself," I said.

"Well, no."

I would not allow myself to be put off by the hurt in his voice—I had *told* him not to buy it for me. "You can't go buying me everything I happen to admire in storefronts."

"You said you liked it. It was on sale."

I refused to take the bag from his hands. "I told you I didn't want it."

"Okay, okay. So I bought it for myself. Are you happy?"

I took the shopping bag. "We'll both wear it. It's great." In stony silence Larry walked on.

The next day we flew to Bordeaux and rented a car. Larry took the wheel first, as we drove east into Périgord, the high limestone plateau that forms the interior of southwest France; Eleanor's Aquitaine. Larry was quiet; he was smarting still, I could tell, from our argument. I had rejected not just a shirt but one of his finest qualities—his generous heart. At the same time I understood that his gifts were not entirely guileless. It was an unhealthy symbiosis: In holding back I gave him reason to feel insecure; for his part, he was trying to buy my commitment, by placing me in the awkward position of having to reject his generosity.

Once outside the city I rested my hand on his knee. "You know why I resist your gifts."

"No. How about cluing me in."

"I can't afford to return your gifts. 'Not having anything to offer, I shall accept nothing,'" I said, quoting Sir Gawain.

"We've been through that. Besides, *I* enjoy buying them. I get pleasure from it. If nothing else, let me have that pleasure."

"I'm too proud."

"Get over it."

"Fine," I said. "But being proud is what keeps me writing, among other things. If I weren't determined to prove myself *to* myself and to others, I might never have taken up writing, and I'd surely have quit by now. It's a package. You love me for my independence and my willingness to take risks—the same things that make me uncomfortable accepting gifts when I can't return the favor."

We drove east, until the road narrowed and the iron-stained limestone cliffs of Périgord began to rise up on either side. "Besides." I forced myself to speak.

"Besides what?"

"Gifts carry love. Each time I accept your gifts I'm committing myself more deeply to being here for you, for whatever happens. And I want to be here for you. But I live in terror that I won't have the courage to honor that commitment. Your gifts remind me of my terror of my own weakness."

We drove the road to Sarlat in silence.

As I write, I have maps spread before me: the marvelously detailed Michelin maps of Midi-Pyrénées and Provence–Côte d'Azur. These we used on that second tour of France, this time through the southwest, east from Bordeaux into the rugged countryside of the Dordogne and the Grandes Causses, south from there to the walled city of Carcassonne and the pleasant Provençal towns of Arles and Avignon.

Like Kentucky the year before, France was in drought during that bicentennial summer. The map recalls long July days with no humidity, the rich earth crumbling to dust beneath our feet, the cold shock of the clear, fast-flowing Dordogne as we stopped by a roadside to take a swim, picking a careful path across fields to the riverbank (farmers there seem unaware of the American obsession with property lines). Or: the two of us standing on an old bridge above the slow, green Vézère—this river might have been transplanted from my childhood in the Kentucky hills, including the archetypal cable-and-girder bridge of memory.

That evening we dined *en plein air* on the terrace of the Madeleine, our hotel in Sarlat, where we ate course after course of the food that the French leave Paris to seek out. Across the square a fountain burbled amid a classically French garden, a geometric pattern of petunias and marigolds and canna lilies, all flawlessly aligned, with the fountain posed exactly in the middle. Overhead the swallows of Sarlat swooped and dove around the medieval houses.

The light was long and low—Europe is on the latitude of Labrador or the Alaskan panhandle, and the summer sky was blue until well after ten in the evening. The service was impeccable, the waiters wearing starched white shirts and dark pants and bow ties (no coats—this informality was allowed, waiting tables outside in the summer). Sitting on the terrace of the Madeleine, Larry and I dined late into that evening. More black-tied waiters in their white shirts appeared, silver-plated crumbers in their pockets: "*Avez-vous choisi, monsieur?*" ("Have you chosen, sir?")

At dinner that first night I wore the black bicentennial shirt. This was by far our most elaborate dining experience, but by now I'd become adept at watching and imitating Larry. Faced with the daunting array of after-dinner cheeses, I learned to ask of the waiter, "*Pouvez-vous conseiller quelque chose?*" ("Can you recommend something?") Ordering the wine, settling the bill—these I left to Larry, to his fluent French and European charm. My own French improved by the day, but I still hadn't the confidence to deal with the unpredictable. I approached each encounter, no matter how commonplace, by practicing phrases in my head, only to panic when reality inevitably departed from my preplanned script. From time to time Larry coaxed me further from my American shell, but like most turtles I was timid, ready to withdraw at the first hint of challenge.

A bottle of Château Poyaune and an Armagnac later: The sun had set, but the sky was still filled with blue light, a Magritte painting against which the swallows swooped and dipped. I understood the perfection of these moments. I was consumed by the consciousness of their slipping away, the desire to hold that moment, not for a day but for an hour, for fifteen minutes, this perfection prolonged; and in its stretching out maybe a hint of miracles to come.

The moment slipped away. The sky darkening, darker, dark, the swallows returned to their nests, the evening gone and nothing to do but hold in the heart the poignance of its passing.

XI

At home in San Francisco: Larry's cat, Willy, was aloof. Left in the care of a roommate who gave him food and water and not much else, he'd become all but feral.

He was a black cat, with three or four white hairs at his throat. He had been a homeless waif—Larry had adopted him at the city pound when he was a few weeks old.

There are dumb cats and smart cats; Willy was a charter member of cat Mensa. At times of his choosing he would chase and fetch curled pipe cleaners, bringing them (trailing dustballs) from under the couch or behind the bureau and dropping them in the lap for another round of pitch and fetch. On days when he felt especially generous-hearted he'd catch a mouse in the backyard, delicately extract its entrails, and deposit the corpse, a tender little gift, in the middle of Larry's pillow.

He was of the school of cats that love having their stomachs rubbed. If in his judgment he'd not received enough petting, he'd reach for the petter's hand with his paw (taking care to keep his claws retracted) and pull it back toward his head. After an especially luxurious petting session he'd crawl up my stomach, to grab the tip of my nose between his teeth for an always gentle love bite.

When Larry and I returned from our second trip to France, Willy recognized us—he gave out his peculiarly plaintive meow the moment he heard our voices at the door. But rather than greet us he ran out the back door and disappeared into the yard. He was missing for hours.

Larry searched every nook and corner. "He's a cat," I said. "He'll be okay. Take my word for it. Cats are always okay."

"But he's done this before," Larry said. "He's pissed at me for being gone for so long. So as soon as I come home, he gets himself in trouble. Last time I had to rescue him from under a neighbor's truck." Finally I persuaded him to come to bed.

In the middle of the night we heard Willy's yowl. Larry got up to investigate.

Willy had gotten himself onto an impossible gable of the roof. From there he peered down at us, intermittently yowling. Neighborhood dogs began to bark. I was wearing nothing but a T-shirt and underwear. It was cold. I was cold. "He got up there," I said. "He's a cat. He'll get down. Let's go to bed. If he's not down tomorrow morning, we'll deal with it then."

Larry was not to be consoled. "The little beast." He sighed. "*My* little beast." He hauled a ladder from the basement and propped it against the wall. It was a shade too short to reach the roof, and when Larry climbed to its top step, Willy backed out of arm's reach. Larry climbed down.

Since I was taller, I took my turn, climbing to the very top rung and reaching out. "Willywillywillywillywilly," I sang, Larry's characteristic call, but the cat backed farther away. I grabbed a nearby gutter.

"Be careful!" Larry cried.

Using the gutter as support, I kicked and clawed my way onto the roof. "The little son of a bitch," I muttered. "*Our* little son of a bitch." I chased him to the roof's edge and grabbed him, wedging him under one arm. He sat there quietly until I hung myself over the gutter, my feet searching for the ladder's top rung; then he began yowling and clawing. I dropped him into Larry's waiting hands and climbed down the ladder, my arms scraped and bloodied from Willy's claws and the roof shingles. Inside, Willy immediately curled up at the foot of the bed and went to sleep, while Larry disinfected and bandaged my arm.

Back in Larry's arms, falling asleep despite my smarting cuts and scrapes, I thought this: *We build our love less on vacations than on midnight rescues of the cat.*

XII

In mid-November Larry and I attended the memorial service for Michael, the good friend and creative writing professor who'd once intervened to help me get a teaching job. (As I type this, I stop to wonder: How is it possible to comprehend or measure this kind of loss—the loss in kindness and help that I would have received from friends had they lived?) Michael had died, of course, of AIDS—he was fifty-four years old. We gathered at a Jewish memorial chapel, where we offered testimonials to him and sat as an elderly cantor with the richest of tenor voices sang the kaddish.

As I sat in the chapel, it occurred to me that once again gay men are on culture's cutting edge, however sadly and inadvertently. Some parts of the service in which I was participating were ancient, drawn from traditional Jewish memorials. At the same time the service as a whole was entirely new, fabricated by Michael's friends from elements of other services we'd attended as gay men in the age of HIV. The circumstances demanded rituals, but we'd been abandoned or ignored by the institutions whose place it was to provide them. So we made up our own: Bring a flower. Read from something the dead person liked. Take home with you some small thing that had belonged to the deceased.

Listening to Michael's service, I considered this: that as the Baby Boom ages, more and more of us, straight and gay, are being called upon to mourn—gay men are hardly alone in being bereft of rituals through which to give voice to our grief. Sitting in the Sinai Memorial Chapel, listening to the haunting kaddish, I considered: What happens to all that energy of grief (Larry's phrase welled from memory) when people have no way to give it voice? Where does it go?

I thought back to the Catholic funerals of my childhood. There's something about seeing—actually *viewing*—a corpse that brings home the fact of death; "closure," a Californian (such as myself) might call it, which is ironic, since it's arguably Californians who have eliminated funeral rituals. Now here we were, the bunch of us gathered without Michael, dead as he might be, as the anchor for our grief.

There are plenty (including, from what I knew of him, Michael himself) who'd find the presence of the body gruesome. And yet for me the body stilled by death underscores the necessary and vital fact of death in life.

I've heard this argument made, that in some measure Western man's lack of respect for the living earth—for its resources, for our human place among them, for life itself—has its roots in our lack of respect for the dead, since it is to the dead that we the living owe our lives.

Exactly one year before Michael's service, on a late-autumn visit to Kentucky, I'd taken a car into the hills, looking for the gravestone of one of the men killed in the sporadic wars between the hill families and the state police. I went to Holy Cross Church, where I'd never before set foot, no matter that it is ten miles from where I grew up.

Holy Cross is the loveliest of a series of lovely, early-nineteenth-century churches that the Catholics built in this small valley. The church sits on a slight knoll, raising it above the surrounding fields—site of the first Catholic church west of the Appalachians, built in 1787, according to the historical marker; the present church dates from 1825.

Unlike most American churches (but like many European village churches), Holy Cross Church sits in the midst of its graveyard. It's built of red brick, in the simplest of cruciforms, decorated only by curving lines of brick laid into the masonry façade. These curves are echoed in the curving lines of the wooden bell tower, painted white and topped with green shingles. The effect is that of an American primitive architecture, created by people who had no formal architectural training but who were first-rate craftsmen and who, in their simple way, took time and patience to create something beautiful and in harmony with its surroundings—the brick was fired in Kentucky, from the same kind of clay that underlies this churchyard. Looking at the church, it's easy to see how it's of a piece with the land on which it sits.

The churchyard was filled with black walnut trees, which on that early-winter afternoon raised bare branching silhouettes against the sky. Spongy black walnut shells were scattered among the tombstones, leaching purple-black stains onto their limestone and granite. From the churchyard I looked down to the hamlet's single intersection (the "holy cross"), where limestone rocks unearthed by the thrifty gravediggers had been used to build retaining walls and a shrine for a plaster statue of the Virgin.

As I stood in the churchyard amid the graves of families whose names I'd never even heard, in the graying winter light, with the black branching limbs of the walnuts and the gray-bleached bones of an abandoned farmhouse silhouetted against the steel blue of the surrounding hills—a sense of sadness, of loss, pervaded everything.

I went inside the church to light a candle. I lit it and made a wish—on that November visit, a little more than a year after I'd first met Larry, I wished for the first time that things might go as well as they could for him, that if worse came to worst, he would have a quick and painless death, with me nearby.

Now Larry's heaving shoulders jerked me back to the present, sitting in the Sinai Memorial Chapel, mourning our friend. For the first time, I saw Larry seized by great, heaving sobs, all the more affecting because he was trying to hold them in. I put my arm around his shoulder. Michael, the man we were memorializing, had been a gay man, a Jew, and a teacher—I understood why Larry was so deeply moved.

And then the service was over and we were outside in the low-slanting, bright, late November sun. Larry was quiet on the drive home; I took his free hand in mine. Driving through these familiar streets, thinking back on Michael's service, thinking back to my journey to Holy Cross Church, I considered how fitting it was to walk past one's dead ancestors each time one approached the church, symbol of spiritual life; how our secular, city lives are empty of these reminders, both of where we've come from and where we're headed. How might we think differently about, say, AIDS, or breast cancer, if the thousands who have died were buried in the city centers of San Francisco, New York, Washington? How might our attitudes toward life change if—as in so many cultures, including the rural culture in which I grew up—memorials to our dead were visibly present among us?

XIII

Over Christmas, Larry's low-grade fevers returned. Each afternoon he took longer and longer naps. His T-cell count continued its steady slide downward; shortly before Christmas his doctor told him he had too few T cells to bother counting. "Anyway, we're not placing all that much faith in T-cell counts as an indicator of health," the doctor said. He continued prescribing AZT in doses much higher than what other doctors at the time commonly prescribed, until finally its side effects (anemia, loss of muscle strength) became too significant to ignore. He switched Larry to ddI, then an experimental drug.

Larry brought the first batch of ddI home with a sheaf of papers requiring his signature and that of a witness. He tossed them on the table and went scrabbling in his room for a pen. "You're not going to read them first?" I asked. "For all you know you could be signing away your life."

An uncomfortable silence, in which he took up the papers. " 'I hereby absolve my health care providers of any and all responsibilities,' " he read. " 'I understand that the drugs prescribed are experimental in nature. They may produce undesirable, unknown, and/or unpredictable side effects, including weight loss, anemia, nausea, headaches, muscle spasms, irreparable nerve damage, pancreatitis . . .' " He read on, into a comprehensive listing of the plagues of mankind, " 'up to and including death.' " He looked up. "A most undesirable side effect." He signed with a flourish, then handed me the pen.

The ddI came in packets resembling Kool-Aid and required a full twenty minutes of stirring to dissolve in a glass of water. "Stir-crazy," Larry called this latest addition to his daily routine, as he cha-cha'd around his apartment to the tinkle of the spoon against the glass. Each day when Larry took up a packet, Willy dashed for the bedroom, where he hid under the bed until the tinkle of the glass and Larry's dancing ended. Then he'd emerge with dustballs clinging to his fur. "The living dust mop," I said pointedly.

"*Somebody's* got to clean under there," Larry said.

That Christmas Larry gave me another Italian sweater, this one more glamorous than practical—it sagged at the neck and bunched at the seams from the first time I wore it. I gave him a floor lamp, which I disguised as a scarecrow in drag, patching together a dress from the scraps of designer wrapping paper I'd saved from each of his gifts. I drew a grinning face on a paper plate and taped it to the lampshade, then molded arms and hands from aluminum foil. In each hand I placed a bouquet of flowers. I posed it at the door, arms and flowers extended, then called Larry to come over to my apartment. When he opened the door, he leapt back in fright, but once he realized what it was, he grabbed his camera and took picture after picture until I made him stop.

"I modeled him after you," I said. "Larry Rose, Dora Maar of postmodern deconstructed furniture-as-sculpture. *Man, with Flowers.* My man with flowers."

"*A* man with flowers," he said. "Not that I object."

I pointed out the handmade dress. "So enough of the jokes about my saving wrapping paper. It's just another part of my ongoing art project. Life as sculpture."

"That's why I love you," he said. "Because you save wrapping paper."

Did Larry's willingness to put his heart on the line grow from some knowledge that this might be his last chance for love? Partly. Did the growth and depth of my affection for him have its roots in some unreconstructed Catholic martyr complex that drew me to the wounded and dying? Partly. But now I know in my heart what before I understood only in my head: We don't fall in love for reasons. This is the source of love's meaning and of our obsession with it. In an age where every phenomenon is assumed to have an explanation, love keeps us human; love taps us into mystery, into that which we can't control or explain: love, and grief.

To love is to willingly lower our defenses, a terrifying prospect in any time and place but especially so at a time and in a place where we perceive ourselves as having so much (HIV; violence; social, cultural, environmental degradation) to defend ourselves against. To love is to give oneself over to another, to entrust to someone else a power that all good sense would have us reserve to ourselves. So we give away some part of ourselves, to find that part returned to us tenfold, in ways we could never have predicted and cannot rationally understand. Loaves and fishes. Miracles happen.

A few miles north of Gualala, on the Sonoma/Mendocino coast, sits a funky resort, a cluster of six cottages, each built more or less a decade apart, constructed as successive owners could afford to add to the property. Taken together they form a kind of living museum of no-tell motel architecture from the 1940s to the 1980s. Larry and I preferred the 1950s tract cottage (pale yellow Formica countertops flecked with gray, matching linoleum, avocado kitchen appliances, three-way lamps hanging from reticulated arms) to the 1960s imitation ship's quarters (macramé wall hangings, a fake ship's steering wheel in the center of the room, beanbag chairs). Mostly we liked the hot tub, cut into a wall of cliffs high above the Pacific. Seals and sea lions barked below. During winter storms the water in the tub sloshed about in sympathy with the ocean, while the wooden deck trembled from the waves pounding against the rocks tumbled at the base of the cliff.

Early in 1990 we spent two nights there, intending to settle once and finally the question of our living together. I taught an evening class, then Larry picked me up and we headed north on Highway 1, into a winter rainstorm.

Larry had begun to show signs of easy exhaustion, so I drove. Rain came in dark, opaque curtains; at times I lost sight of the edge of the road in the darkness of the storm and the night. More than once I was grateful we were driving north, hugging the cliff, driving the inside lane.

> And they are gone: aye, ages long ago
> These lovers fled away into the storm.

The next day the sun shone with low brilliance, with the clarity that comes only in wintertime in a marine environment where the wind sweeps clean and clear across the ocean. Larry and I climbed down a ravine to the beach, then he ran ahead, to the foot of a rocky promontory.

Along this northern California coast the continent is not so much meeting the ocean as throwing itself headlong into the sea. High and steep, the cliffs are composed of crumbly shales and serpentines. Wearing tennis shoes, Larry started picking his way up a cliff that I would have thought twice about climbing wearing hiking boots. I started to warn him, then held my tongue. I watched him climb higher and higher, until he reached and perched on a rocky ledge. "I'll turn you into a country boy yet," I called up from the beach. I snapped a photo of him, clinging precariously to the rock, grinning in triumph.

That night we read aloud "In the Ravine," Chekhov's story of Lipa, a peasant woman beaten down by fate and the indifference of humankind, who survives through the simple power of her will to endure. We took turns reading this long story until we neared its end, where I took the book from him to read one of my favorite scenes.

Lipa has lost her only child, who died after her jealous stepsister scalded him with boiling water. Walking home from the hospital, Lipa encounters an elderly traveler breaking up his nighttime fire.

"I have been at the hospital," said Lipa after a pause. "My little son died there. Here I am carrying him home."

. . . The old man picked up an ember, blew on it—only his eyes and nose were lighted up—then . . . he went over to Lipa with the light and looked at her, and his look expressed compassion and tenderness.

"You are a mother," he said; "every mother grieves for her child."

. . . "My baby was in torment all day," said Lipa. "He looked at me with his little eyes and said nothing; he wanted to speak and could not. Lord God! Queen of Heaven! In my grief I kept falling down on the floor. I would be standing there and then I would fall down by the bedside. And tell me, grandfather, why should a little one be tormented before his death? When a grown-up person, a man or a woman, is in torment, his sins are forgiven, but why a little one, when he has no sins? Why?"

"Who can tell?" answered the old man.

They drove on for half an hour in silence.

"We can't know everything, how and why," said the old man. "A bird is given not four wings but two because it is able to fly with two; and so man is not permitted to know everything but only half or a quarter. As much as he needs to know in order to live, so much he knows."

Larry held up his hand. "Read that again." After I'd read it a second time, we lay for a moment in silence. "That's so wise," he said. He leaned back against the bedstead, his hands behind his head; big-armed Larry.

I butted him in the side. "Scoot over. This pair of queens should insist on rooms with queen-sized beds."

"Will you make me a promise?" he asked. "Will you promise to visit my parents?"

The room, the world around the room, grew still. The ocean tossed itself against the cliff, the waves still excited from yesterday's storm. "I don't much believe in promises. You know that already," I said finally. "I do what I do, and you love me for who I am, and I love you for who you are, and we live in the here and now. Who knows what next year is going to turn up?"

"They really don't have much of anyone. Not many young people anyway, besides me. And you."

At some place I knew this was the beginning of something, that things were turning and I did not want them to turn, I wanted them to stay in this present moment, in this cramped bed with the patterned polyester bedspread and the ocean's sounding below the window. "Look," I said. "I'm sure I'll stay in touch with your parents."

"That's not the same as promising you'll visit them."

"I won't promise something I can't promise, can't you see that? If I happen to go to Los Angeles, and I do every once in a while, I'll give them a call and maybe if I get some time free and I'm on the west side, I'll drop in. But I can't promise I'll visit them because I just don't know what my life will bring. Who knows where I'll be in a few years. I might take a teaching job back East—that's possible. Anything is possible. But I don't make promises unless I know I'll carry through on them. You know that. And right now, right here, I just don't know."

Silence.

"Larry. I have seven brothers and sisters and their in-laws and a widowed mother and fifteen nieces and nephews, for God's sake. Almost all of them live on the other side of the continent, and I don't see any of them as much as I'd like. It might be easier for somebody without all that family. But for me, it's too much. There are limits on how much love I can give."

He stayed in my arms but turned away. We went to sleep that way: I unyielding, he disappointed, both of us terrified by the implications of what he'd said.

The next day we walked up and over the cliffs to a small headland jutting into the Pacific. We sat amid a grove of pines and clowned around. He took more pictures: several of me with my shirt off, my chest winter-bare and lit by the January light skating off the Pacific— this place, this California where in January I took off my shirt and the sun felt warm and good. The air was washed clean by the rain, the horizon was a razor-drawn line; far out at sea we saw an occasional puff of mist—gray whales spouting. Tiny puffs followed larger puffs, the adults heading south to winter in the Gulf of California.

We picnicked, another of Larry's outdoor feasts: French pâté, San Francisco sourdough, prosciutto, dry Jack, Joseph Schmidt chocolates, a young but pleasant Napa zinfandel, of which Larry drank only a glass. Afterward we lay back, staring into the trees. A pileated woodpecker flew from a branch, its eerie cry rising and fading as it passed overhead, and in that cry I heard something of the irrepressible continuity of life and the terror and beauty and necessity of death, and I turned to him and said, "Why not."

"Why not what?" he asked, though I could have meant only one thing.

"Why not move in together."

As I write this, I'm struck by the gap between romance and reality, between my fantasy even now of how such a conversation "ought" to have happened (violins, lit candles revolving in the sky) and the sadness that accompanied the real thing. A smaller-hearted man than Larry might have demanded more enthusiasm on my part—he *wanted* those violins and revolving candles—but he was satisfied that he had won his cause. "That would be great," he said, nothing more. Whether because of his illness or as a gift from his parents or both, he understood what I had yet to learn: that joy is a gift with which it's stupid, maybe downright evil, to argue.

On our last night at the Gualala resort a second, weaker but colder front swept through. We drove back to San Francisco underneath the redwoods bordering the Navarro River, through the vineyards of the Anderson Valley, through Boonville and over a small pass in the coastal ranges. As we gained elevation, the drizzle turned to snow. Bared of their leaves, the gnarled trunks of the grapevines were ranks of gnomes, an army of vineyard spirits whose shoulders had been dusted by some heavenly confectioner.

Descending the Waldo Grade from the Marin Headlands to the Golden Gate Bridge: The hills were taking the first blush of that Day-Glo California spring green. The city stood etched white against blue across the strait.

"About moving in together," I said. "I don't believe in placing conditions on decisions. But. I have a condition. We know how this disease progresses. I'm not revealing any big secrets, we've both seen it happen. You might end up in the emergency room and it will be left to me to call your parents and tell them why you're there. And I can't take responsibility for that. You have to tell them yourself. You owe that to them."

Traffic slowed, then snarled as the freeway narrowed. The bridge was gridlocked. With his free hand he reached out and took my hand in his. "I'll tell them."

"I'll help. I'll be glad to help. It will be an honor to help."

He rolled open the car's sunroof. Stuck in traffic, we craned back our necks to follow the art deco sculpture of the bridge towers to their tops, golden red against the sky's cloudless winter blue. This was a different city we were returning to, a city that we claimed together.

XIV

Within a week of our return from the Sonoma coast, Larry had registered us with an apartment-search company and was poring daily over the classified ads. I humored him, though when we were together, I managed a lot of thinking out loud: I was in the middle of teaching and too busy to think about moving, I was working on a feature article and too busy to think about moving, more places will open up in the springtime, we should wait and move then. He nodded and kept searching.

Within two weeks he located a spacious apartment in Bernal Heights, a kind of Brooklyn for San Francisco, brought to some semblance of toniness by the views from its northwest slope and its proximity to other, more fashionable neighborhoods. This street was occupied by a very San Francisco mix: aged Italian ladies, the neighborhood's first residents, who'd moved here with their families in the 1920s, when dairy cows still grazed the hill. Bikers who'd scored on a big pot deal in the 1960s and used the proceeds to buy a house in this then-cheap neighborhood. Gay couples in long-term relationships—men who'd grown to resemble each other, living next to lesbians in painter's pants. A sprinkling of Latino families who'd wandered up the hill from the Mission District. Yuppies who liked the neighborhood for its ease of access to the freeways leading south to Silicon Valley.

The landlady demanded a credit check. Larry's (A+) ran to four pages; mine (A+) was one line. "Good thing one of us participates in the consumer economy," I said. On the strength of his lifetime of shopping she agreed to rent us the place.

Ten A.M., February 13: The landlady called and arranged to

meet us that evening at my apartment, so that the two of us might sign the lease. I called Berkeley High School and left Larry a message: *All systems go.*

Eleven-thirty A.M., that same day: Larry phoned back. "I'm seeing things in my left eye. I'm going to the emergency room as soon as school's out."

That afternoon he called from the hospital. He'd been diagnosed with CMV retinitis. Since CMV is categorized as an opportunistic infection, the diagnosis carried with it the official label of AIDS, and while the label changed nothing about the facts of Larry's condition, it ruled out any pretense that somehow he might be spared the fate of the other HIV-positive men we knew. Treatment was with DHPG, a drug administered intravenously and so potent that it quickly destroys the vein into which it's fed. He would require a catheter installed directly to the heart, where the volume of blood dilutes the drug's immediate potency. He would have to administer an IV daily, sometimes twice daily, "for the duration of his illness"—which was to say, the duration of his life.

I arranged to pick him up at the hospital. I'd planned to buy a bottle of champagne to celebrate our new apartment. Now, it seemed, fate was offering me a last chance to reconsider, to back out; we had not, after all, signed the lease.

I bought a bottle of Veuve Clicquot, Larry's favorite.

Later that night, after our future landlady had come and gone, Larry lay in bed, glum. He drank only a sip of champagne, leaving me to consume, more or less, the bottle. "I'm pissed," he said.

I waved the half-empty bottle. "No, I'm pissed."

"You'd think we'd get—"

"You'd think we'd get," I said, and lay beside him.

I am an indecisive man, a border stater, child of Henry Clay and John Breckinridge, "almost a Libra," someone once told me pointedly; slow to decisions, weigher of all options.

"But you're a Scorpio," the same, astrology-crazed person told me. Once the cards are cut, I never abandon the table, regardless of the deal. And I had opened my eyes this much, to begin to understand that I was in the presence of a great lesson and a great teacher, and that I had embarked on a great adventure, however fraught with sadness. Surely one definition of love is its power to bring us out of ourselves, to force us to venture beyond what we've accepted as our limitations.

I raised my glass. "*Bons baisers,*" I said, and we kissed.

The CMV/AIDS diagnosis forced the issue of telling his parents. He frequently made the short trip to Los Angeles to visit them, and the complications and machinery of the daily IV treatments would be impossible to conceal. We arranged to visit them early in April. He would fly down on Friday and tell them of his illness; I would follow the next day.

I cannot remember why we made this somewhat unorthodox arrangement—why we did not arrive together to tell them; possibly because we acknowledged Larry's closeness to his parents and the particularity of the histories that bound them together. Larry would speak German in telling them of his illness. My presence would require simultaneous translation, difficult to imagine under such charged circumstances.

The only child returning to tell his aged parents that he will die before them: Poetry might do justice to such a moment, or music, or opera, their combination; but prose fails—my prose, at any rate; or maybe just my imagination.

When I arrived, the warmth and resonance of his parents' greeting made clear that my place in their eyes had been strengthened, both by what Larry had told them and by their understanding of the importance of a partner in facing such battles.

Larry cheerfully set about engaging his "drip," as he'd nicknamed his daily IV treatment. Kathy and Fred spoke with forced amiability. We spoke of his illness as if it were an imaginable thing, an object as ordinary and mundane as the coffee table or our glasses of water. Then Kathy made an excuse to take me into the back-yard. We stood blindingly lit by the unmediated southern Califor-nia sun, amid flowers already in riotous bloom. Kathy wept bitterly, as I stood stone-faced and rock-silent, fighting my own terror and feeling acutely the inadequacy of anything I might say.

I did not understand then that there are times when presence is all we can ask for, all we can give. At such moments words trivial-ize. We can only stand together, offering the touching hand, the lit-eral shoulder to cry on; the comfort of our mute presence, company in the dark.

In that small house I felt both suffocated and liberated by love of such intensity. In loving Larry I had been touched by the literal hand of God, for that is what love is. In his mother's eyes I was transformed from a rival for Larry's love into an ally. To his father I became, not just a friend to his son, but a genuine son-in-law. Because of AIDS his parents welcomed me into what had been a nearly closed circle, a family unit walled off from the harshness of history. Because of AIDS I became a member of the family.

Early that spring I wrote to my mother:

> My deciding to take care of Larry as he goes through
> this is in part a religious decision—a decision to thank
> the power, or powers, that have granted me life. And
> it's a humanistic decision—a storing up, I can hope, of
> grace; if I stand at someone's side during this hard por-
> tion of his journey, perhaps, I can hope, I will have
> someone to stand by me when my time arrives, be that
> one or five or fifty years away. I know that this is not
> how things work—there is no justice or fairness in life,
> none that we can count on anyway—and yet I have
> enough Catholic in me to be superstitious, and enough
> of your pluck in me not to care: to decide to throw

myself in the face of fate and good sense because, I
guess, of love.

These were the bad months. The fevers and chills that developed
shortly after Larry's diagnosis with CMV worsened, mysteriously
peaking shortly after each IV treatment. Sometimes he went
straight from his IV treatment to bed. He took a leave of absence
from teaching, a step we were careful to call temporary.

Larry visited his doctor, who shrugged. "You have AIDS. People
with AIDS get fevers." On the drive home I argued for the first
time for switching to a new doctor, but Larry resisted. He'd been
seeing this doctor for several years, he wasn't one to change horses
in midstream, he believed in Western medicine. And he was
afflicted with a kind of fatalism that I knew and understood. In his
case its roots lay in Judaism, in my case they lay in Catholicism—
which is to say, one tree branching from another's roots.

Then this dinner party, the thirty-second birthday of a friend.
Before the meal we gathered in front of what our host presented as
his "home entertainment center"—the largest television I'd ever
seen, a compact-disc player, VCR, cassette deck, a laser-disc player. He spoke easily of how two years before he'd had KS lesions
removed from his leg, and they'd yet to reappear. Since then he'd
been living on disability insurance, which sweet, impractical Larry
had never thought to acquire. He was full of health, our host, and I
could not help but think, *Why should this man have such health when
Larry is so sick?* "I have a friend who's just gone on ddI," our host
said. "But his T-cell count is rock-bottom—thirty or so." Larry
hadn't seen thirty T cells in six months.

Joining us for this conversation was another of our friend's
friends, a man so emaciated as to define life-in-death. He was not
there, not present with us in any real way. At supper he ate—his
appetite seemed unaffected—but he carried no sentence through to
its completion. His thoughts were not with us but with the dead.

Eight or ten of us sat at the table: cheery banter, but none of the usual birthday jokes about getting older; those jokes left gay men's conversation some time ago. I raised a toast to the head of the table, to the birthday boy. Midway through the toast I noticed that eyes were looking elsewhere. By the end of the toast I noticed that conversation had faltered, but the circumstances were strained and who could fault the conversation for faltering?

Larry tapped my arm. He was sitting on my left, away from the birthday celebrant and out of my line of sight, and so I'd not seen what others were pretending not to notice. "I'm shivering again," he said. Within seconds he was seized by chills so violent he slipped and fell from his chair. I insisted on leaving—unbelievably, he demurred ("after the others finish eating"). I insisted, he refused, though he was betrayed by the chattering of his teeth. Some of the guests tried to sustain some semblance of conversation, some were quietly staring at their plates. Only the death's-head of a man continued eating in his painfully slow way.

Finally Larry yielded. He could not descend the steps—he was too weak—and so I half-helped, half-carried him to the car. He would not go to the hospital, a premonition of his later refusal to seek care whose significance I was too dense to grasp.

I took him home, fed him hot water, put him under the electric blanket, climbed into bed to warm him with my body. After a while his shivering stopped.

The next day I took him to the hospital emergency room, where the attending physician immediately recognized the periodic chills as symptomatic of an infection in Larry's catheter. Each time he administered his IV drug he was spreading the bacteria through his system—thus the quick rise in fever and chills an hour or so after each IV treatment. A large dose of antibiotics and the fevers disappeared.

I argued again for a different doctor; Larry dug in his heels. He was as stubborn in his own way as I, and better at manipulating events to get what he wanted.

We moved into the new apartment and still Larry could not summon the energy to return to his job. One day he'd feel fine, and he'd clench his fists in frustration that he'd decided to stay home. The next day he could barely stand up and would sleep fifteen or sixteen hours. Enough of these days and he quietly extended his leave of absence through the remainder of the semester.

His desk began making a transition. On one side, stacks of junior English papers bleeding red ink fought for space with grade books, well-thumbed texts, and lecture notes. On the other side, pale blue forms from insurance companies were rising in a growing, lopsided mountain. In between were hypodermics, cotton swabs, latex gloves, bottles of disinfectant, sympathy notes from his students, and presiding over all, the silver IV pole.

I came home one evening to find him reading a letter he'd received from the girls (there turned out to be two culprits) who'd once hidden mash notes in his faculty mailbox. One had flirted with us on the day I'd spoken to his class, two years earlier. Now as seniors they sent him Shakespeare's Sonnet #78, which Larry had taught to them; a poem about (among other things) the relationship between teaching and love. On the outside of the envelope they listed their addresses and the colleges they'd be attending in the fall.

Larry began hooking up his IV. "My students must have figured something out. They all send sweet notes, but none of them says 'get well.'"

I pointed at his IV. "Teach me how to do that."

He shook his head. "You might stick yourself with a needle."

"Nurses do dozens of them every day. What they can learn, I can learn."

He snapped on latex gloves, swabbed his arm with orange disinfectant, poised the needle. "I'm wondering if I should tell my students about my diagnosis. It seems like the best possible way to educate them about the disease. But then I think about what happened with all that anti-Semitic stuff." In his first years as a teacher he'd received death threats, notes left in his mailbox calling for the "kike fag" to quit or suffer consequences. Finally he found a note bearing swastikas and reading, "Jew Fag Will Die." At his insistence the school called in the FBI. With his father's help Larry hired an attorney to pursue the case. Ultimately the school persuaded him to take a semester's leave with pay—it was during those months that Larry spent his longest stay in France. But the school never identified the criminals, and Larry carried with him the memory of those times.

I thought of the inevitable stress of telling his students, and Larry's increasingly fragile health. "You can tell your students," I said. "You should tell them. But you should do it when you go back, when you can plan how you're going to do it, instead of just dropping this bomb through a phone call or a one-day visit."

"You really think I should wait." He sounded both disappointed and relieved. He found the catheter port and slid in the needle, then opened the valve from the IV. "Bingo. First try. Maybe you should watch me more often."

To add to his problems, the IV medication was far from trouble-free. He'd had a subcutaneous catheter installed, which required that he stick the IV needle through his skin. On many days, even with frequent tries the needle would not find its target, and Larry would curse in frustration. Once I found him weeping, his arm bloodied from repeated failures.

Gifts took on ominous implications. I bought him a cassette deck to replace his old one, which was broken. I couldn't afford the deck—two years earlier I'd never have bought it—but now I thought of Larry and bought it on impulse. I bought it by way of cheering him up, but we both understood its implications: long days confined to the house, in need of entertainment.

The semester played itself out. Larry did not return to his job.

In June I called our friend Fred, at whose house Larry and I had first met. I invited him to accompany us on a picnic. On the phone he sounded distracted and disorganized, though he was enthused at my invitation. But on the day of the picnic itself, he never appeared.

A few days later I heard that Fred had been in the hospital but was now at home. I went alone to visit him; Larry was feverish and afraid of passing along a flu or a cold.

Fred was Jewish and a Southerner, giving him access to two great traditions of hospitality. In the 1970s he had hosted Gatsbyesque parties that began when Saturday night's revelers gathered to watch Sunday dawn from his hot tub and stayed late into the afternoon to watch the fog pour over Twin Peaks. In the 1980s he threw his house open again, this time for so many memorial services I'd lost count.

At his home, Fred was bedridden and long gone into dementia. He'd not spoken a coherent sentence since shortly after my picnic invitation. Once he'd been a passionate devotee of opera; now music caused him physical pain. A single note—the ringing of the doorbell—and he screamed in agony. He answered questions in unintelligible barks. He had not eaten in a month and was starving to death. When I tried to touch him, he shrank away—touch brought him pain.

I took the back streets home, a long drive, and as I drove, I prayed this: God in heaven, we cannot ask that you ordain what we wish, but have mercy on this man I love. Spare him, spare me watching such a death.

At home Larry asked after Fred. "I'll go visit him tomorrow."

"I don't think that's a good idea. I'll let you know if he gets better."

Larry did not press the point.

In the middle of that summer Larry regained some measure of his prediagnosis strength. Every day he rose later and later and napped in midafternoon, but we went out in the evenings to plays or movies and visited friends. I began to think fondly of our idyllic summers in France. Now we had come together in love; we were inhabiting the same place at the same time. On our earlier visits to France I'd understood the beauty of these trips, but I wanted to return fully cognizant of the magnitude of the gift I had been given. I wanted to break one of life's inexorable laws: I wanted fully to appreciate the meadow before it became a parking lot; I wanted to know and honor the man I had before he was gone.

I decided to take that autumn off from all responsibilities, quitting my teaching job. I told Larry that my goal was to finish my second novel, though inwardly I knew that I was quitting so as to have time to care for him. Now it was my turn to suggest we go to France. It's time for another vacation, I argued, not acknowledging that it would almost certainly be our last.

Larry had doubts: The complications of the IV treatment, which he would have to lug across an ocean. The exhaustion he felt even on the best days. And what if something went wrong? "We'll deal with it," I said. "They have hospitals in France. It's not like they're strangers to AIDS." I had a vision of us in that autumnal light, in what we knew was the autumn of his life, and while we could not maintain the pace of past vacations, I looked forward to a journey during which, instead of museum-hopping, we relaxed in cafés or spent hours on park benches watching the pigeons in the Tuileries. Larry was unconvinced.

In August his health worsened. He had more fevers now; he spent whole afternoons in bed. Boils began to break out on his skin, growing overnight to cherry-sized, filled with pus and lymph fluid. I quietly dropped my suggestion of going to France, which now seemed wildly impractical. I began to speak instead of a vacation in America, Hawaii maybe—a vacation with no city stress, where we might lie on the beach, where touring was not a possibility.

Toward the end of that summer I was working late. We'd had supper and I'd returned to my desk to spend another hour or so working on an article. My office looked west to a panoramic view of the bowl of San Francisco's Mission District and Noe Valley, sweeping in a patchwork of pastels to Twin Peaks. The moon was a silver crescent, setting as the sun set, caught in the horns of the television broadcasting tower that tops the hills. I went to fetch Larry to come watch.

He was hooked to his IV—there'd been evidence of increased viral activity, and his doctor had placed him on twice-daily treatments. I sat next to him on the couch, which he'd bought to celebrate our making a home together (he had insisted, of course, on buying the biggest and most expensive one). Willy, the cat, often slept in Larry's lap while he administered his IVs, and now he stirred and stretched his claws.

As I sat, Larry looked up. He lifted his arm, dangling its IV tubing. Willy struck at the tubing with one lazy claw. "I'm dying," Larry said.

And I, the great pragmatist, the invincible confronter of reality who had for the duration of our time together been pushing him to exactly this acknowledgment—confronted with the bald fact of things, I lost courage. "Oh, but we're all dying," I said—a miserable memory.

"That's not what I mean." I sat next to him and held his hand, until his IV finished and the beeping of the computerized pump broke our silence. "Let's go to France," he said.

Over the next week we discussed the trip. With a stubbornness I was beginning to understand as a family trait—the stubbornness that surely kept his parents alive through the Holocaust—Larry now insisted that he could make the transatlantic journey. Even as we discussed the pros and cons of the trip, I overheard him making plane and hotel reservations, phoning his French friends, making appointments with his doctor to discuss the logistics of traveling with IV medication.

These were months of joy. After all my reservations at our incompatibility, we had settled into domesticity as if we had been lovers in some previous life and were now taking up where we'd left off.

I had moved into the new apartment first, with my few possessions; Larry's task was not so simple. Each evening he tackled the mountain of papers, paraphernalia, memorabilia, and junk that he'd accumulated. Each day I moved a few more of his boxes. When time came for him to move, he was in the midst of his fevers and chills, but I took advantage of my flexible schedule to move his things.

This was exactly what I'd feared—that his illness would consume my time, that I wouldn't be able to work. But now the wonderful thing made itself evident: I took enormous pleasure in doing these things for him. Each day he struggled to do the work of moving, but his strength was clearly inadequate to the task. Each day I admonished him for trying, until I started making excuses to stay at his apartment through the morning, surreptitiously taking charge of the sorting and packing so that Larry might sleep in.

The movers balked at the sight of Larry's bedroom. "I ain't never seen this much junk," one said. When they moved Larry's bureau, one leg broke under the shifting weight of all those expired batteries, bars of soap, and bottles of Vetiver cologne.

During these days I was teaching, finishing an article, running a grant-making program in the arts, working on my second novel, trying to clear my desk before the trip to France and in preparation for an autumn given over entirely to Larry. He was overjoyed at my success, even as his own days became a progression of fluctuating fevers and IV treatments, doctor visits and endless paperwork.

Established in the new apartment, we settled into a pattern. Each day I rose early and worked at writing until noon. In mid-morning Larry joined me for a cup of coffee and to listen to my complaints about a churlish editor, a stubborn manuscript, a character who kept slipping from my grasp. We ate lunch together, after which he napped, then hooked up his drip, during which he read or filed paperwork. (An hour and a half daily was just adequate to keep him abreast of the mounting stack of medical forms.) We took turns fixing supper. In the evenings we sometimes went out; more often we ended each evening reading aloud to each other.

To celebrate our moving in together I brought him flowers—not for the first time, but that particular evening I decided to imitate the approach I'd seen him take at the florist. Rather than buying a single bunch of whatever looked fresh, I assembled a bouquet: daffodils, irises, gladiolas. I chose them with some trepidation (*Wouldn't it be wiser to leave this to somebody who knows what he's doing?*). At home I arranged them in a vase, the yellow daffodils and cobalt irises and scarlet gladiolas, a brilliant assemblage of the primary colors of spring. On the table I assembled a flotilla of various small animals done in wood or ceramic, gifts from Larry since our first months together. Then I centered the vase in their midst.

Larry, of course, grabbed his camera, making me mug with the bouquet. "Everything I know I learned from you," I said. "Except for the gladiolas; those I learned to like from Miguel," my old roommate. When time came to throw the flowers away, I looked at their withered stalks and realized how much truth my casual remark contained.

In the middle of that summer, a longtime college friend and his wife had their second child, a girl. Larry and I went to the hospital for a visit.

The room was filled with the joy and pride and relief that accompany the birth of a healthy baby. Unlike most of my friends, I'd been present at any number of such scenes—as youngest of a large family, I had visited sisters and sisters-in-law after their babies' births. Now we were enacting that old ritual: handing around the newborn so that each of us could coo and tweak her cheek and let her tiny fingers close around our own.

I passed the baby to Larry. "Can I hold her?" he asked doubtfully. "Of course," the mother replied. He was ecstatic. My friends did not suspect the source of his appreciation. Of course we all knew the facts—there was no danger here—but the newborn seemed so fragile, especially to Larry, for whom holding a baby this young was a first-time experience. Later he told me that the readiness of our friends' trust gave him as much pleasure as the joy of holding their daughter.

Around the same time, two of my San Diego nieces, both aged eight, came to visit with my mother and two of my sisters. Larry drove them around San Francisco, showing them sights and places (Fisherman's Wharf, Lombard Street) that I considered too crowded to visit, and which my nieces (of course) loved. Then I drove them up the coast, where my car's battery died. Larry postponed a doctor's appointment to come to our rescue.

They fell in love with him; they fell in love with us as a couple. "Uncle Larry" my nieces called him, an honorific he surely earned.

Once back in Kentucky my mother mailed me a St. Christopher's medal. "Give this to Larry," she wrote. "Tell him I'm praying for his health."

XV

Over my time of knowing Larry, Willy had gone from being a tomcat in his prime to being something of a grande dame in black fur (frost-tipped now with a little gray) who turned his nose up at catnip toys and curled pipe cleaners and spent his days tracking the sun from window to window. He was a big fan of our sessions of reading aloud; he curled up on Larry's lap, or if Larry was lying down, on his stomach.

In the middle of that summer of our third year together came Larry's turn to choose what book we read aloud. He picked García Márquez's *Love in the Time of Cholera*.

I balked for a moment at its heft (350 large pages of small print). But I had arrived at this superstitious conclusion, born of my Catholic fatalism and my love of books: So long as we were in the middle of a book, he wouldn't die. The longer the book, the better.

Love in the Time of Cholera is set in an unnamed Colombian coastal city (Cartagena?). The book opens late in the life of Fermina Daza, on the day when her doctor husband falls from a ladder to his death. Fermina rushes to her husband, lying on the patio beneath the treacherous ladder.

> She prayed to God to give him at least a moment, so that he would not go without knowing how much she had loved him despite all their doubts, and she felt an irresistible longing to begin life with him over again, so that they could say what they had left unsaid and do everything right that they had done badly in the past.

I paused after reading aloud this invitation, courtesy of García Márquez, to speak aloud my own heart. I had so much to say to Larry: how deeply I had come to love him, how profoundly he had changed my life, how in each other we had found our traveling shadows, how big was my fear of his death.

But anything I might say would only remind him of his illness, I argued to myself. To make some extraordinary declaration of love now would only draw attention to his weakening.

And so I read on, into Fermina's days after her husband's burial:

> Her grief exploded into a blind rage against the world, even against herself, and that is what filled her with the control and courage to face her solitude alone. . . . Everything that belonged to her dead husband made her weep again; his tasseled slippers, his pajamas under the pillow, the space of his absence in the dressing room mirror, his own odor on her skin. A vague thought made her shudder: "The people one loves should take all their things with them when they go."

"I think I'll stop there," I said.

XVI

With a growing battery of drugs, Larry's health stabilized, but for inexplicable reasons his salivary glands shut down, making a chore of eating, once his great delight. Each day he slept longer and longer, and we began to miss performances or dinners we both wanted to attend. The inevitable day arrived when I snapped at him for some minor delay. After a few minutes he went outside on the deck. I followed him out to find him sobbing. "I'm so tired of being sick," he said, and though it wasn't the first time he'd said that, it was the first time he'd revealed it with such passion. His saying as much underscored for me how much staying alive is a matter of will—if you don't have much interest in continuing to live, you have a reasonably good chance of making good on your intention.

Now, Fred, our friend, was not likely to live much longer; his death would signal the end of an era of my life. Those first years of coming to San Francisco, the first years, really, of coming out, of making peace with being gay—gladiolas and opera, discos and drugs, those will have wound to an end, and hardly in the way anyone might have expected. Of my old circle all would be dead except me.

Around me I saw this happening: People keeping up with one another largely because they're all HIV-positive; banding together out of mutual affection, of course, but also out of commiseration. And then I saw new crowds of gay men who hadn't had many contacts with the epidemic, for whom it has been a distant phenomenon. And passing between those groups, people like myself, HIV-negative but bound to the dying by ties of affection and memory. AIDS involves a premature aging—I saw this happening to

Larry, in the crow's-feet at his eyes, in the parched skin at his temples. But the aging extends beyond those who have the disease. I felt like a much older man, watching the world I took for granted drop away person by person. One day I phoned my seventy-five-year-old mother and listened to her talk of singing in the choir for the funeral of one old friend after another, and as she spoke, I thought, *Yes, I know this place. In my late thirties, this is where I am.*

Late that summer, on an evening when Larry wasn't feeling good enough to go out, I made a brief visit to a friend's birthday party. We sat in a circle, eight gay men. They asked after Larry, then the conversation turned to the latest drugs and alternative therapies. For the next hour my friends compared their experiences with acupuncture and Chinese herbs and AZT and ddI. All their conversational signals pointed to including me in this, the least enviable of fraternities. They did not know my HIV status; I felt hopelessly constrained from revealing it—who would be so crude as to raise in this company the subject of his own good fortune? Sitting among these friends, I felt like an eavesdropper, a fraud, as if I were pretending to a sorrow I hadn't earned; even as I was consumed with despair at the prospect of watching these men die, helping them die, losing my life to them, losing them from my life.

Another day I was describing Larry's symptoms to an HIV-positive friend. I spoke of the difficulty of straddling the need to accept his illness in our lives and the need to live some kind of life apart from it. "This is the place we've been brought to," I said.

"*He's.*"

I looked at my friend quizzically.

"It's the place *he's* been brought to," he said. "It's not your disease. It's not your death."

A dozen versions of "Yes, but" came to mind. I left them unsaid.

That summer the International AIDS Conference took place in San Francisco. Larry and I marched with thousands of other people down Market Street, calling for more research funding and an end to discrimination against HIV-positive people. The conference was at the Moscone Convention Center, where Louis Sullivan, Health and Human Services secretary under Reagan, was scheduled to speak. Led by ACT-UP, the marchers waited there to protest the administration's refusal to acknowledge or act against an epidemic that was continuing to spread even as it was entirely preventable.

Larry and I had participated, together and separately, in various peaceful demonstrations, but we'd always stopped short of any disruptive action. Larry had continued his volunteer work at the AIDS Foundation. I was active in various gay arts and political organizations, all of which had issues surrounding HIV high on their agendas. I was writing about HIV-related matters. We'd discussed our admiration for demonstrators who engaged in civil disobedience, even as we agreed that each of us was fighting his own battles, in ways that were different from in-the-streets action but no less important.

In front of the convention center I waited with Larry and our fellow demonstrators, but Sullivan was late, no doubt by design. After several hours I returned home, anxious to get back to writing.

I worked through that sunny afternoon and into the evening, until I began to worry—always conscientious with his medications, Larry had missed the appointed time for his IV treatment. Almost at sunset he burst in the door. "We took over the hall!" he cried, trembling with excitement. "We took whistles and pans and sneaked past building security, and then when Sullivan started to speak, we blew whistles and drowned him out." He rushed to the television set. "I want to see this reported."

There they were, the lead story on both local and national news. "I was down front," Larry said proudly. "Practically in the first row."

"Did you consider any other tactic?" I asked. "Like standing in silence and turning your back?"

"Been there, done that. We wouldn't have gotten his attention or anybody else's by standing and turning our backs."

"What about Sullivan's right to speak?"

"He has the power to speak anywhere, anytime he wants. He has a responsibility to speak, and he's saying next to nothing. Since *he's* not saying anything, *we* have a responsibility to speak."

This was a side of Larry I'd never before glimpsed—the dramatic opposite of the obedient son; a man energized to act, to seize and declare his rightful place as participant in the social contract, even at the risk of condemnation and arrest.

I was uneasy at his decision, but I withheld my arguments. I had never seen Larry so excited, so invigorated, so vastly sure of himself and his rights as a citizen. In the glow that he carried for days afterward, I came to understand the importance of action as the tangible manifestation of hope, and the way in which hope, along with courage, is as powerful as any drug in sustaining life. Touched by his action, I began to think about my own responsibility to act, not only in large public ways (writing, speaking), but in the ordinary events and among the people of my daily life.

That September I flew to San Diego for a weekend visit to my sisters and nieces. On the plane I sat in front of a black couple and a white woman. From the first safety announcements and into the journey south, the white woman chattered at her seatmates in a voice projected at her surrounding passengers. She was a Christian, she claimed, associated with the Riverside County Board of Mental Health. In that capacity she dealt with a range of "troubled people," including homosexuals. She talked about how "they" are winning "the battle against children," but how "you'd be surprised at how many there are who are sick of 'them' "; how she'd listened to a "recovering homosexual" speak, how important she found his message, how fond she was of that term: *recovering homosexual.* "It's a disease, you know," she said loudly, "that you can get over as surely as you can get over the flu, if you put your mind to it."

Imprisoned in my seat, I was enraged. Some portion of my

anger came from my situation with Larry, watching his courage and knowing his fear and his family's fears, and my inability to vent my own anger and fear at watching him dying. Part of my anger came from the helplessness of my own situation. When I told people I had a lover who had AIDS, I heard in their voices the assumption they leapt to: that I myself must be HIV-positive, that I myself must be on the verge of death, because why else would I stick with a man dying of a communicable disease? Each time I felt defensive, torn between the urge to say, "Oh, but I'm HIV-negative," and the feeling that it was none of their damned business; that their place was to educate themselves in the workings both of HIV and of love.

As I sat imprisoned in my plane seat, all the voices of my childhood clamored in my heart: *Keep quiet. Mind your own business. Everyone has a right to his or her opinion. Don't rock the boat. You're not a real man anyway. Your opinion is less than worthless.* And in conflict with those distant voices I heard the voices of my more recent past, the voices of my friends, many now dead; Larry's voice: *I'm dying.*

And so at the end of that San Diego–bound flight I stood and spoke with my best Southern charm, but my voice trembling with rage and terror, not at speaking out in public but at speaking out alone; the plane's engines stilled now and the plane silent except for the opening and closing of luggage compartments and a scattering of low-voiced chatter. "Ma'am, I'm sorry for listening to your conversation but I have to speak," I said.

"Oh, I know I'm a loudmouth," she said.

"No," I said (meaning *yes*), "no, ma'am, but as a gay man—"

As soon as I said the forbidden word, the midsection of the plane grew quiet. To a person the passengers froze in the midst of their packing up and turned to listen. "You are hurting people by what you say," I said.

"I'm sorry if I hurt your feelings," she said smoothly, the apology practiced to perfection, the beat not missed, forgiveness earned by a few easy words.

I exploded then, my voice a controlled and trembling shout.

"Don't apologize to *me!* Think about what you're saying and its effect on people, especially a young gay man or lesbian who might hear you, and how bad it would make them feel about themselves." My passion bristled in the still, stale air.

"I will," she said stiffly.

"Well, I appreciate that," I said, and turned to my luggage.

Everyone resumed packing, but in silence now, the air charged with emotion—what *power* words have! I think on this as I look back. A single word—*gay*—spoken with passion, had transformed this mundane plane ride into an event.

The doors swung open. Passengers began moving up the aisle. The idle postflight chatter resumed, though quiet and hushed—we were nice people, uncomfortable with such public displays of passion, especially when cooped up in surroundings that enforce routine politeness.

The self-described Christian turned to her seatmates. "They're such a difficult problem," she stage-whispered.

Moving up the aisle and into the rest of the day I was a jumble of emotions: pride that I had brought myself to speak at all; shame that my residual self-hatred and self-doubt had tied my tongue, that I had not thought to say all the convincing, perfect arguments that moments later flooded my head.

I left the plane, to be greeted by my family. I hugged my sisters and nieces more warmly than usual, partly because I was hoping the woman whom I'd confronted might witness this display of family love; mostly because I felt so acutely the preciousness and perfection of their love, given so unconditionally.

Late that summer, after a courtship as determined and almost exactly as long as Larry's courting of me, my mother accepted the marriage proposal of her Southern gentleman, now eighty-four. He phoned each of her eight children to ask for our permission. In turn, my mother wrote each of us letters asking what we thought.

I replied:

I admire you for taking on the burdens and responsibilities of a relationship again. Surely the easiest thing
to do would be to stay single. But just as surely, life is
defined by the living. As long as you're sticking your
head out, something will happen to it one way or
another, and while you may get it chopped off, by my
own money that's preferable to using it to model hats.
(And now that hats are out of style there's no place
even for that.) You can fade with the wallpaper or you
can get out and hit the dance floor, and looks to me
like you're doing the latter.

Of course, hitting the dance floor has its troubles
and heartbreaks. This is what we learned from you,
which I've taken as the governing principle of my life:
it's better to take a risk and lose than never to take a
risk at all. Now, please don't tell me that's foolish—
I'm not sure I could change my ways, at this late date.
If you think I've completely misinterpreted all the education you gave me, it's probably best just to allow me
to continue in my ignorance. But I think I learned this
from you.

Meanwhile, it looks as if Larry and I may go to
France. To France? What a strange notion. I have told
Larry that I'm afraid we're plunging ahead with this
trip because we believe that once abroad we will leave
all this behind—that we will step off the plane at
Charles de Gaulle and Larry will be the man of two
years ago, and all this illness will seem distant, impossible. The fact is that the real course of events is likely
to be more grim and more fraught with danger and
exhaustion, and yet we forge ahead.

XVII

During the day Larry slept. I worked most of the morning, then peeked into the bedroom to find him still asleep—ten hours, twelve hours asleep, only to wake exhausted and wanting more sleep.

We were far along in reading *Love in the Time of Cholera*. I was troubled by how quickly a book passed when we read in it every night. I did most of the reading now—Larry was too weak—and I was reading slower, because I'd become obsessed with the notion that Larry would not die so long as we were in the middle of a book. I didn't want this book to end; I wanted Florentino Ariza to get Fermina Daza, his life's love, yes, but I wanted them to travel forever up and down their magical tropical river, however it had been ravaged by very contemporary, very real clear-cutting. I wanted them to travel forever and I wanted Larry and me to travel with them, since as long as we were traveling, we were a moving target, as long as we were on the road, he was alive.

"There are things," Fermina Daza says, "you only do for love." I read this to Larry. Then I read, " 'The weak never enter the kingdom of love, which is a harsh and ungenerous kingdom.' " And, " 'Nothing resembles a person so much as the way he dies.' "

We were nearing the end of the book. We were in the midst of our discussions over whether or not to go to France and I saw the end of the book coming, and before we could finish it I raised the question of what we were going to read next. "My turn to choose," I said.

"Something it would be fun to read in France."

"We don't have to go to France. We could stay here in America. We could stay in California."

"I want to go to France. How about a book about a journey?"

"A long book. *Remembrance of Things Past*. All seven volumes."

"I don't know about that. I like the idea of reading something French, but that's too long."

"I'm just kidding."

"How about *Madame Bovary*?"

I stared in disbelief. "You, the original Francophile, have never read *Madame Bovary*?" I rejected his choice. "You should read it on your own, but it's too grim to read aloud." We settled finally on Homer's *Odyssey*, the quintessential road story, which Larry hadn't read since college and which I'd never read.

And then we were on the last pages of *Love in the Time of Cholera*, we were staying up late to finish it. Willy was happy about this. These days I called him our elder states-cat. As Larry had become more bedridden, Willy had become more domestic, spending nights sleeping at our feet and days sprawled at Larry's side.

" 'It is life more than death which has no limits,' " I read, only a few pages from the book's end. " 'Love was always love, any time and any place, but it was the more solid the closer it came to death.' "

At my insistence, we started the *Odyssey* the same night we finished *Love in the Time of Cholera*.

XVIII

Before leaving for France, Larry and I met for a last time with his doctor, who encouraged us to make the trip. In my head I listed all the signs of Larry's worsening condition: the fevers, his exhaustion, the boils on his skin, which were increasing in number and size. Each night I laid my head on his chest, to hear his heart beating in a wild, shallow fibrillation. As the doctor was winding up our appointment, I spoke to him of these and other symptoms. He brushed them aside. Larry had only to take care not to overtax himself, he said.

I remonstrated with Larry on our drive home, but he was stubborn. "We can do it. I feel fine."

And so we packed for our third journey to France. What was an afternoon affair for me became a weeklong process for Larry, as he assembled needles and IV bags and catheters and swabs and disinfectants and pills, all the paraphernalia that accompanies a patient in the advanced stages of AIDS. All this he crammed into a vast suitcase, whose contents he was still sorting and organizing less than an hour before our departure. I surveyed our bed, strewn with medications and medical equipment. "We could pack this in the car and head north, a few pleasant days in some Sonoma County resort. Everyone here thinks we've gone to Europe—we could stay right here in the apartment, we could play hooky in our own city. We could bag it all now."

He mulled this over a short second, then gathered up the remaining medications, dropped them in the suitcase, and closed the lid. "You sit on that side, and I'll be able to get it shut."

"If you want to go," I said, "I'll go with you." I sat on the suitcase.

And then we were in France, staying again with Larry's friend. On our first Sunday, I went into Paris to tour alone while Larry rested. Near the day's end I sat in a small park outside the Musée de Cluny, the museum of medieval Paris. I wrote postcards, which I'd bought in the museum gift shop. Each featured one of the museum's six great tapestries depicting the five senses: vision, in which an elegant lady holds a mirror to a unicorn, so that he may admire himself; hearing, in which she plays a small organ, while the unicorn crouches, listening, at her feet; touch, in which she stands with the faithful unicorn at her side, her hand grasping its delicate ivory horn; taste, in which she eats from a bowl of berries; and smell, in which she dissects a flower, petal by petal.

And then the mysterious sixth panel: Beneath a banner embroidered *À Mon Seul Désir* ("To My Only Desire"), the lady removes her richly worked necklace; symbol, perhaps, of her rejection of worldly senses in favor of a more spiritual life. "But I like to think it's a portrayal of our sixth sense," I wrote on a postcard I sent my mother. "It's memory—our sense of the poignance of time's passing."

Larry was late for the rendezvous we'd planned. As the light failed, I grew angry—I was sure he was spending time with his French friends, or on the phone with his parents, but either way this was precious time, the waning of our time together, time I wanted for myself, for us. And then he was later still; it grew nearly dark and my anger turned to fear, and then he appeared. I had seen him coming for a long block, but I had not recognized this bent and hobbling man as my lover.

"I couldn't find the park. I walked around the block and then I got so tired I had to stop and rest a few times."

We took each other's hands and sat together for a while in silence.

Larry stood first. "I want to show you the shops on the Boulevard St.-Michel. Maybe I'll find you a birthday present."

We walked along, looking in the windows. "There's a nice jacket." Larry took my hand and stood me in front of the store window and sized it and me up. "You'd look good in that. We'll come back and check it out." We were drawing stares now, and I remembered stories of gay bashings along this street. At the same moment we wordlessly dropped each other's hands; Larry had been thinking of the same danger. We did not take them up again that night.

The next day we walked in the Jardin du Luxembourg, where elderly ladies once charged a few centimes for the privilege of occupying a bench. "France is changing. Even France," Larry said, though the canna lilies and marigolds were as symmetrical and brilliant as memory might want. From there we walked to the church of St.-Sulpice.

Inside, Larry sat to rest, next to two impassive Frenchwomen in dark suits, kneeling and fingering their rosary beads. I approached the great statue of the Virgin, standing atop the immense pregnant globe of the world. Illuminated from a hidden window, she was splashed with sunlight so that she glowed as if lit from within. She floated above the world and its troubles, cradling in her arms the child, while crushing beneath her delicate heel an enormous conger eel of evil: the archetypal image of virtue triumphant.

I chose the longest, ten-franc taper and lit it with the prayer that by then had become my interior mantra: *Let him die a speedy death, a painless death, a death with me at his side.*

As I touched the match to the wick, I heard his sobs, deep, heaving sobs of the kind I'd heard him cry only once before, at the memorial service of our friend Michael. I returned to his side.

"I saw you lighting candles and thought of you and your mother lighting candles for me, now and after I'm gone."

I wrapped my arm around his shoulder. The women drew away. I pulled him closer and kissed his cheek, oblivious to their scorn.

To cheer Larry we walked from St.-Sulpice to Angelina, the legendary tea shop with its luscious pastries and (Larry's favorite) hot chocolate, so thick we ate it with spoons. From there we crossed the

Rue de Rivoli to the Tuileries, where we strolled in the autumn's dying light, the light for which we'd come to Paris, this year-end light filtered gold and streaming the length of the Champs-Elysées. In this sunset hour we sat on a bench. "It's so beautiful here," Larry said finally. "I'm so lucky to be here with you."

I looked at my watch; I had no choice. I was the guardian of his health. "And we're so late. If we don't get to Châtelet soon, we'll miss the last express to the suburbs, and that means waiting an hour in the station." I gathered our things. "We can stop along the way. But we need to get you home early. We've already done too much for one day."

Near the Châtelet station Larry saw a shop featuring Irish sweaters woven in intricate patterns. "Let's check these out. I might need a new sweater this winter." As soon as we were inside, he searched out sweaters for me to try on.

The salesgirl was a young, cream-complected French girl with high cheekbones and dark eyes. I looked longingly at a sweater she retrieved from the back room, an Irish hand-knit, blue-green with green geometric patterns. "I'll buy it for you for your birthday," Larry said. "It's only a few weeks away."

I checked the price tag—it was the most expensive item in the shop. "Oh, let's look some more," I said. (Still—so late!—I had not learned my lesson.) "I might see something else I want. We can always come back here, it's so close to the station." Reluctantly Larry let her replace the sweater, and we left the store.

On Wednesday I rose early and went alone into Paris to the street market at the Rue Mouffetard, a small street complete with an organ-grinder accompanied by a monkey and a miniature goat. The fish markets featured whole octopus and squid, mussels, coquilles Saint-Jacques by the hundreds; pancake-flat sole, both eyes staring upward; rose pink salmon; and enormous, boa-length eels, as thick as a large man's thigh, arranged as if frozen in the act of swimming.

Next door the meat market carried whole, furry hares hanging from racks, ducks still feathered, and a single flayed head of lamb, its tongue arranged as if poised to lick the sheepherder's hand. Each woman carried a basket—there were few men in this street, at this early Wednesday hour—and each had a small mutt on a chain, that she led (or was it the other way around?) as she went about her purchases. Those beautiful fish! I wanted to live here only so as to be able to cook them.

I took the train back to the northern suburbs to meet Larry. That evening we returned together to the city, to the Hôtel Salé, the Picasso Museum, open late on Wednesdays.

We had the museum almost to ourselves, the benefit, finally, of being in Paris off-season. Unlike most French museums the Hôtel Salé has many benches, and we went from room to room sitting on each for a bit, looking at paintings. "Such beautiful paintings!" Larry exclaimed. "How wonderful to sit with you among them!"

Afterward we sat in the courtyard of the Hôtel for nearly a half hour, so that Larry might rest for the journey back. In that half hour only one couple came into the courtyard, two young artists dressed in the obligatory black and delighted when we told them that tonight was *gratuit,* free. We sat watching the light fade from the sapphire sky, and it was as if we had all the beauty of Paris to ourselves. I felt these words welling up in me, I fought them back because of their finality, but they wanted to be spoken aloud and finally, remembering Fermina Daza's regrets at the side of her dead husband, I yielded to their insistence. I turned to him and spoke my heart, as he had taught me to do. "I'm so lucky."

We sat in silence, our arms around each other, watching the light fade from the sky.

Knowing that I loved the French countryside, knowing how I loved to get out of Paris, Larry insisted that we take a trip out of town, though by now he could barely walk the several hundred yards to the suburban train station. "You've never been to Nice," he said. "It's so beautiful. I could show it to you."

The idea was lunatic—the plane trip, the trek to find a rental car, checking in at a hotel, all that walking. I was becoming acutely aware of all I took for granted, chief among this being the ease with which I walked everywhere, anywhere, at will.

I persuaded him that Nice was too much of an expedition. The next day I returned from a trip to the market to discover he'd made reservations at the Hôtel Jean Bardet, one of the best hotels in the Loire Valley, with a two-star restaurant. I tried to discourage him, but again he insisted—he *wanted* this journey, by now he wanted more than I to be together again in the French countryside.

I sat on the floor and leaned my head on my knees. "Why are we going on this trip? Not for me!"

"Well, if you don't want to go, then we don't have to."

In his resignation I remembered my place on this journey. I lifted my head. "If you want to go, I'll go with you."

And so we went to Tours. That morning, a Sunday, he could barely walk, and so I helped him down the stairs. He leaned on me for the short walk to the train station. The train into Paris, a cab across Paris, the wait at the Gare Montparnasse. With each walk he weakened, with each I had to help him a little more. On the train to Tours he fell asleep. Then the arrival in Tours, the renting of the car, the drive across town to the Hôtel Jean Bardet: Each step was a triumph, each step was closer to something that he wanted, and because he wanted it, I wanted it for him.

More manor than hotel, the Jean Bardet contained the world in its intensively cultivated gardens. One corner was a formal French garden, with the usual regiments of canna lilies and marigolds marching in file. In another corner a barnyard held geese and ducks and guinea hens, some of which were destined for our supper. To one side there was a fallow field, at the foot of which grew a huge kitchen garden, with the late-season vegetables (peppers, tomatoes, eggplant) still proliferating and herbs still in bloom. At the base of the sloping garden grew a small forest. All these were visible from our second-floor room.

Larry was momentarily dissatisfied. "I told the clerk I wanted a room with a single king-sized bed."

"You didn't really think they'd put two men in a single bed."

"We're paying, they should give us what we want."

"You've been around me too long. That's the most American thing I've ever heard you say."

Larry hooked up his IV and we hung it from the top of the French doors. We sat outside on the balcony, watching the sun set over the gardens while the IV dripped.

We'd made a dinner reservation at eight. Larry was exhausted from the journey but insisted on having dinner. "Take a warm bath," I suggested, drawing on folk medicine I'd learned from my mother, a country woman with too many children to afford a doctor. Larry still mistrusted my folksy advice, but to oblige me he undressed while I ran the water.

The tub was larger than the bathroom of my old studio apartment. Larry was too weak to sit or stand on his own, so I sat him in the warm water. I sponged his shrunken hips. The boils that had begun to break out before our departure and that his doctor had dismissed as insignificant were multiplying. I soaked each with a warm cloth until it broke, then drained it onto a clean cloth.

In this gesture I understood in some small way the love that motivates women and men who give their lives to the weak and ill. I understood the shallowness of my fears that I might abandon Larry once he grew sick. Now I wanted only to be with him and to care for him, for in caring for him I was caring for myself. I discovered that I loved even his illness and his dying. How to explain this to someone whole and healthy? I loved his illness and dying because they were a part of him; there was no having him without these. It was no longer given to me to have him whole and healthy; very well, I would be satisfied with having him weak and ill.

I dressed him for dinner. He was too weak to pull on his socks. In tugging them over his feet I noticed his ankles' swelling; it was during this bath that I was struck by the realization that though he'd been eating very little he'd lost no girth. "You should see a doctor," I said. "Tours has become a big center for medicine. We can find a good doctor here."

But he refused, and I acquiesced. I didn't know what the swelling might mean, and after all, his doctor had so vehemently assured us that all would be fine. And the surroundings were so perfect. Who might imagine a worm amid this paradise?

Because of a hundred bicyclists visiting from Paris, we ate not in the nicer dining rooms (reserved for the bicyclists) but in a room that was far too bright, too light, too spare. But the food was offered and served with the flair and choreography one would expect of a two-star restaurant. The sommelier visited to present us with the lengthy wine list. Larry could no longer drink wine, and I did not want to drink a bottle alone. I looked over the half-bottles, a meager selection.

The sommelier approached. "*Avez-vous choisi, messieurs?*"

I selected a local red, all that was available in half-bottles. A slight frown of disapproval creased the sommelier's brow; the Loire is not known for its reds, but he bowed and disappeared.

Eating had long since become a chore for Larry; now he was presented with a feast, from which he could manage only a few bites. Instead of the food, we spoke of the choreography, the table-ware, the flowers; these he could enjoy. I had known for a year and more that I would dedicate my second novel to Larry, but I was superstitious about such matters, and I had never told him as much until now, when it was apparent that my chances for speaking were fast disappearing. And so I told him that I would dedicate that book to him.

He was pleased but distant. Already I saw his thoughts grow

more scattered, until his eyes glazed. He stopped speaking in mid-sentence.

I sat watching. For thirty seconds and more he sat in a state of suspended animation, while around us life continued. The sommelier visited a nearby table. "*Avez-vous choisi, monsieur?*" A raucous cheer rose from among the bicyclists.

I placed my hand over his. "Larry?"

He came back from where he had been. Through a visible effort he willed himself back to the meal, back to the here and now, to the world of the living, to the middle of this two-star meal with its retinue of waiters and me at his side.

"We should leave. You're not well." Again I suggested going to the hospital in Tours.

"No," he said. "I want to finish dinner. I want to be here with you."

"We should leave," I said, though I quailed at the thought of announcing this to our entourage of waiters and then walking, carrying Larry, through the mob of bicyclists.

Our waiter appeared, his forehead wrinkled with genuine Gallic concern. "Monsieur does not like the dish? Perhaps I may bring something else?"

"*Non,*" Larry replied. "*J'ai peu faim, c'est tout.*"

After this he sneaked his food from his plate to mine. I ate two meals of the world's most lavish food, until mercifully the meal was over.

Climbing the stairs, he needed my support, gladly offered. As we climbed, the night manager stood at the foot of the stairs, giving us the first of many disapproving looks.

The next day I ate breakfast in the glassed-in dining room and declined an invitation to reserve a table for that night. The manager was cool—I suspect she thought we, among the Bardet's youngest guests, had found it too expensive for our budgets.

Larry rose around ten. I gave him another bath, but this one less elaborate—I was impatient to spend time with him away from the treatments, the boils, his exhaustion.

And so we took our last drive, south and west along the banks of the Loire, and the beauty of that day endures. The Loire was a broad, silvered mirror to our left; the colors of the sky slid lazily among its shallow rocks. On our right stone-walled villages and fairy-tale castles backed themselves against the hills and limestone cliffs and the shivering yellow poplars. This was the geography of my first visit to France—as a college student I'd lived in the Loire Valley—and at every bend in the road I met ghosts of my young self: on a bike tour, going wine tasting, drunk on being young and alive in a foreign country. Now I was older, here again; this time in love.

I drove until I was blinded by tears—Larry was so quiet, so ill. Outside of Langeais I stopped the car and asked, "Are you in pain?"

"No."

"We could turn back."

"I'm happy being quiet here with you."

In Langeais, we stopped in a small restaurant across from the château, where they served the simple country food that the French should be more famous for—neither rich nor heavy but hearty and well prepared. We ordered a thin vegetable soup, the only thing that Larry could eat, served with *crème salé,* salted cream (which he refused—another sign that things were off, wrong).

And then we drove on. I was thinking this, and finally I spoke it aloud: "We could keep driving. I want to keep driving. We can just go on, and leave all this behind, and just keep going. Bordeaux, Spain, Africa."

But we reached Chinon, the sun was sinking, I checked the map: we would not encounter another bridge for many miles. We crossed the Loire and turned back. On the south bank, next to the bridge, sat a massive nuclear power plant, its fences rusting, its concrete shell chipped and decaying. I thought how much I needed to see this tangible evidence of human frailty and mortality amid this otherwise perfect countryside.

We stopped at Azay-le-Rideau, most beautiful of the châteaux, but Larry was too weak to walk the grounds, he could not lift his feet and so we headed back to Tours. In its suburbs I lost myself amid a maze of confusing signs. Larry had not spoken since Azay-le-Rideau, and I was frantic at the signs of his growing weakness. In fear I became my worst self, impatient, short-tempered, furious at the French for marking their roads so very poorly, not because we were lost—I would find my way sooner or later—but because I knew, now, that every minute had to count, there weren't many of these minutes left. This holy day was over.

XIX

The sun sat on the drought-parched Loire. In the garden below a small flock of guinea hens, the garden's exterminators, poked and prodded for bugs—funny-looking birds, as if someone had set out to make a chicken but forgot to streamline and color the product. As I looked down from the balcony, all seemed so ordered, so flawlessly arranged: no weeds to be seen, the lawns raked and trimmed and mowed and sloping to a California coastal redwood, a nice incongruity thriving here in the temperate Loire.

Larry sat on the bed, struggling to hook up his IV. He was exhausted from our drive through the châteaux. I tried to persuade him to skip tonight's treatment—surely his rest was more important than one evening's medication missed—but true to himself he was determined to get this IV to work. Earlier I'd sneaked the phone into the bathroom to call his San Francisco doctor, to voice my fear at Larry's worsening condition and to seek reinforcement of my decision to insist that he enter a hospital. The doctor was in his office but too busy to take my emergency, transatlantic call. Now I made a second call.

From the bed Larry asked, "Who are you calling?"

"The American Hospital. I'm taking you to Paris tomorrow and checking you into the hospital." For the first time he did not object, and in his acquiescence I understood how very sick he must be.

I replaced the phone, then knelt to remove his shoes—his ankles were so swollen he could not pull his shoes off without help. I looked up at him, and I understood that time was growing short, what I wanted to say I must say now or risk leaving it unsaid, and so I acknowledged, however implicitly, what we were hurtling toward. "You know I'll never forget you."

And then I was outside on the balcony, watching thunderclouds pile up to the west, their towering heads brilliantly backlit, their bases dark with shadow and rain. The wind picked up, the guinea hens scurried for cover. "Come to the balcony," I called to Larry, "look at the sunset," but he was engrossed with his IV—it was balking, he was having more trouble getting it to drip, and anyway he was too weak to stand and cross the room dragging his makeshift IV pole (a bent hanger hung from a clothes tree).

"It's working," he called. I returned to his side, to read aloud to him while his IV dripped.

All through this journey I'd been reading aloud the *Odyssey*. I had not thought we could finish it on this trip because I had not anticipated how much time Larry would spend in bed, how much time I would spend reading to him. I had not thought to bring an understudy—another book to leap into after finishing Homer. Now I was reading ever more slowly, as slowly as I could, but we had finished twenty-two of its twenty-four books, and this evening I began the twenty-third.

After years of battle in the war with Troy, many adventures and much wandering, Odysseus finally reaches home. There he finds his household overrun with men who assume he is dead, and who have for years sought the hand in marriage and with it the dowry of his wife, Penelope. She has steadfastly refused their aggressive advances. With the help of their son, Odysseus slaughters the arrogant suitors and cleanses the household of their corrupting presence.

But Penelope will not trust her senses, she has given so much time and heart to waiting and to keeping her passions in check; she has exhausted herself in hoping for her husband's return, and she barely recognizes this stranger, so many years gone, so worn and aged. To test Odysseus she tells him he may sleep alone in their wedding bed, which she's commanded her servants to move outside the bedroom. Odysseus bellows in anger—he himself constructed the bed with "an old trunk of olive / [that] grew like a pillar on the building plot" as one of its posts. The bed couldn't have been moved without destroying it.

In his anger Penelope recognizes that he shares the secret of the bed's construction, that he is in fact her long-wandering husband returned.

As I read, I held the book in my right hand. In my left I took Larry's hand, his arm still attached to the IV. The tubing rattled against the bedside. "Where's Willy when we need him?" Larry asked.

To the west thunder rumbled. Clouds had swallowed the setting sun, but this was no real storm—a few patterings in the dust and already the clouds were moving on to some other, more grateful place. A few minutes before the sun set it broke through the clouds, and as it broke through, this is what I read aloud.

> Think
> what difficulty the gods gave: they denied us
> life together in our prime and flowering years,
> kept us from crossing into age together.

But Odysseus faces one last test. He must walk inland, his oar on his shoulder, until he is so far from the sea that the farmers mistake his oar for a plow. There he must sacrifice to Poseidon, the sea god, in thanks for his surviving the journey from the battlefields of Troy.

> Then death will drift upon me
> from seaward, mild as air, mild as your hand,
> in my well-tended weariness of age,
> contented folk around me on our island.

This I read aloud, holding Larry's hand while his IV dripped. Then I read:

Penelope said:
"If by the gods' grace age at least is kind,
we have that promise—trials will end in peace."

· · · · · · · · · · · · · · · · ·

So they came
into that bed so steadfast, loved of old,
opening glad arms to one another . . .
The royal pair mingled in love again
and afterward lay revelling in stories . . .
Remembering
he drowsed over the story's end. Sweet sleep
relaxed his limbs and his care-burdened breast.

I closed the book. "One more chapter left. We have to think about finding another book."

Larry lay back on the pillows, eyes closed. "I liked that part."

XX

The last day, the first day.

No sleep. In the middle of the night I phoned and reached Larry's doctor in his San Francisco office, just as he was leaving for the day. His first question: "How could you let him get this sick?"

The next morning I carried Larry to the car. At the bottom of the stairs the hotel manager and her daughter watched. Arms folded. No help.

In the car: accelerator to the floor. Five hours to Paris. Larry slept. At a stop for gas he tried to use the bathroom. I helped him across the gas station apron but he was too weak to stand at a urinal. Stares, glares, this time from the station attendants.

In Paris: lost, then boxed in a blocked one-way street. Sidewalk driving. Bad directions, then good directions misunderstood.

At the American Hospital: I couldn't locate the emergency entrance. I parked at the main entrance, left Larry in the car, and dashed up the stairs. Three women at the reception desk (volunteers?). "*Mon copain est gravement malade avec le SIDA.*" ("My friend is gravely ill with AIDS.") My words echoed in the small waiting area, or was this my imagination? The low hum of reception-room chatter fell silent. Two of the three receptionists rose and walked quickly into the rear offices. The third rose to follow. "*S'il vous plaît, madame, je vous en prie.*" I was begging now. The silent watching waiting room. The receptionist sat and called for emergency staff. Attendants came with a wheelchair and got Larry from the car.

Across the frantic drive from Tours he had been all but comatose, but now we were at the hospital and the hope of help and the need to put on a good show revitalized him and he walked, leaning on my arm, through the doors and to the desk. The receptionist pushed forms at us. Larry tendered his credit card and signed his name, forming each letter with care and precision on a slip of paper whose carbon sits before me now, years later—even in this, his last signature, the letters might be copied directly from the idealized cursive script posted, white lettering on green background, above elementary school blackboards. In that cramped, perfectly formed hand I read the story of one perhaps too devoted to being the man others wanted him to be; loved, maybe, too much (is this possible?) by parents who had survived the worst where others had not.

The doctors: "*Tout va bien.*" ("Everything is fine.") IVs, private room, then the move to intensive care, waiting. Late in the evening I returned the car to the rental lot at de Gaulle Airport, then spent the night at Larry's friend's apartment.

No sleep.

Next day: I phoned early and reached the intensive care unit's head nurse. "*Monsieur Rose se repose. Tout va bien.*" ("Monsieur Rose is resting. Everything is fine.") Visiting hours would begin at 2:15 P.M. No one would be allowed to see or speak to a patient before then. (Weeks later, back in America, reviewing the computerized, detailed billings, I would discover that he'd had a heart attack in the middle of the night—that he'd died and been revived [*réanimé*] with CPR and electric shock to the heart.)

I paced the apartment—might as well be at the hospital. I arrived there late in the morning and climbed the stairs to the intensive care ward.

Entrée interdite (Entry forbidden).

An American angel hovered at my ear. "Go on in," she said. "To hell with the rules. What can they do but throw you out?"

His bed was straight across from the ICU door. He saw me and struggled to sit up. He tried to say something about the night before. I made him lie down, put my finger to my lips. "They'll throw me out if they see me in here."

They saw me in there. They asked me to leave. I nodded politely and made an appearance of standing. Once they were gone, I sat back down and took his hand.

"*Ne pleure pas,*" he said. ("Don't cry.")

They came back. The head nurse this time, the busty Scotswoman with whom I'd spoken earlier in the day ("*Tout va bien*"). In forceful English she ordered me to leave or she would call hospital security to have me bodily thrown out. I left.

I walked around an hour, two hours. *Je pleure.* At exactly 2:15 I opened the ICU door.

He was in the midst of his second heart attack. I saw the cardiac monitor rise, then fall, 70, 60, 45, 20. The monitor alarm sounded. No one came. I stood frozen, watching, unbelieving, afraid to move for fear of being seen and thrown out. The monitor went dead, a flat line. No one came.

At my ear my American angel spoke. "Keep quiet. Let him die. The man has earned his death."

I waited. I waited. The monitor cried, a harsh flat plaintive hum zero zero zero. No one came.

I moved to embrace him, and in my crossing to his bed I was spotted by the nurses' station. A nurse moved toward me, then noticed the monitor's blaring hum. "*Appelez 84!*" she cried. Several nurses pushed me aside and rushed to his bed. They began the violent dance of CPR. I backed from the room. I had no need to witness this.

Five minutes, ten minutes, fifteen minutes. The doctor emerged. "*Il vit encore?*" I asked, unable to speak in either language any form of the evil word.

"*Non. Il est mort. Je suis désolé.*"

The walls fell away, the floor fell from under my feet, the doctor was no longer there. I was alone, as alone as it was possible to be, falling into a well so deep I didn't know how deep, falling. In this single moment my youth fell away, I was no longer innocent, I was no longer young. I embraced all that I had been given and my arms closed on nothing. Now I was falling free, free-falling, and as I fell, I thought of all those candles lit, all those wishes made—a painless death, a speedy death, a death with me at hand.

At the American Hospital the nurses would not allow me to watch or help as they cleaned Larry after his death. I would not want to see him, they told me, in this state. And I acceded—did I have a choice? They had his body, on which I had no legal claim. While I waited I thought, *I who have bathed his sores, wiped sweat from his forehead, embraced him in passion and in need; I who have in some small way risked my life to shepherd him to this death—I know his body as none of them know it; I want to know it once more, in the time of his death, but I'm denied this. I am, after all, only his friend.*

XXI

The day after Larry's death, sitting in an office in the American Hospital. I'd made the necessary calls: to my mother, to ask her advice on how to break the news; to an aunt and uncle, to break the news to them first so that they might be at hand for Kathy and Fred; last, to Larry's parents. Since arriving in Europe I'd not slept enough to recover from jet lag, and I was acutely aware of the nine-hour disjunction between my body's California time and the industrial-sized wall clock dictating the comings and goings of the place where I happened to be. Sleep? A distant relative whose name I misspell on Christmas cards.

Now I found myself on one side of a U.S. Army–issue desk empty of anything but the oldest and blackest of rotary phones. The barren walls of the hospital room where I found myself had once been white; judging from their discoloration, they'd not been painted since the American expatriates of the 1930s came here for their checkups. On the other side of the desk sat Monsieur Régis Grenier, a man in his midtwenties who not once in our many conversations spoke a word of English. It's possible that he spoke French to put me at a negotiating disadvantage, but I think not. He was a mortician, after all, not an academic or a world traveler. In me he was confronting, possibly for the first time in his young mortician's life, a man who was mourning his male lover, in the American way of grief.

I am grateful to the Catholic Church not for any spiritual assistance with Larry's death but for providing me the means to understand the cultural underpinnings of the greater part of the Western world. In my dealings with Monsieur Grenier I knew already what for those not raised Catholic I should explain, by way of illuminating the war of wills that followed:

Until recently Catholicism strongly discouraged cremation of the body. Church theory contended that on Judgment Day the bodies of the dead would rise from the grave to join for eternity their souls, who had since their bodies' deaths passed the centuries plucking harps in heaven or toasting in the fires of purgatory or hell. The church's theory was that ashes could not rise; therefore, no cremation. My seventh-grade catechism embellishes the point: "Cremation has been advocated by anti-Christians with the express purpose of destroying belief in the immortality of the soul and the resurrection of the body," it reads. That this dogma takes no account of the unsavory actions of worms never proved a problem to the fathers of the church, but then consistency and logic have never been the concern of Catholicism—or, for that matter, any other religion.

And so we plunged into our transaction, Monsieur Grenier and I. We introduced ourselves, we formed our initial impressions. He was thin in the skeletal way of French men, with prominent, elegant cheekbones; he'd slicked back his hair with glistening brilliantine, but it stuck up at its crown with the stubbornness of youth, making him appear younger than he would most likely have wanted. He wore a silk Yves Saint-Laurent suit (thanks to Larry, I recognized the cut) whose color matched the desk's gunmetal gray. I was wearing clothes I had worn for days: on that last drive with Larry along the Loire, on the mad dash from Tours to the American Hospital, throughout the day of Larry's death.

Still, my wrinkled shirt and frank odor were small potatoes, or so I thought, in the face of what Monsieur Grenier and I had in common. We were both nice, white boys. We might assume, or so I naïvely hoped, a certain mutual understanding of the workings of the world. We were polite. We would encounter no problems that we could not work out.

Through our negotiations I came to an understanding, but it

was not the understanding that I had anticipated. I came to under-stand that culture manifests itself most emphatically at times of passage—birth, marriage, illness, death. I came to understand again how irrevocably American I am. As for Monsieur Grenier, judging from his reactions, I suspect that he came to believe firmly in the unfeeling flightiness of Americans.

People are always in danger of being done in by their myths, the more so if they live in California or in France, places that have given over so much energy to creating and sustaining their particular cultural myths that those myths are now the governing MO, the way things get done. Monsieur Grenier and I were playing out our particular myths of death—his French, mine Californian—but with a stacked deck. He possessed the seven seals, the paperwork, the power to release me from this country. I was on his territory, in his country, in his language. And he held this indisputable trump card: habeas corpus, my lover's body.

And so we began. I find it difficult to translate this recollected conversation into English, a language that at its most circumspect is blunt and raw compared to French; but we plunged in, using the tongue of courtship and diplomacy.

Pleasantries, the obligatory desolation (*"Je suis désolé"*).

I opened the discussion.

"Monsieur Rose avait demandé que—" ("Monsieur Rose had requested that—")

I was at a loss for the proper word. No French class or language tape had prepared me for this conversation.

"Monsieur Rose had requested that his body be burned (*brûlé*)."

Monsieur Grenier started, stifled a grimace, then proceeded in a French as exact and impeccable as his suit.

"If I may suggest another choice of words. *Brûlé,* this is for—desserts. The word for which you search is *la crémation.*" (*"Vous cherchez un autre mot, c'est la crémation."*)

"Je vous remercie. Monsieur Rose wished *la crémation.*"

A lifted eyebrow. "But the body will be destroyed."

A pause.

"Of course," I said.

"Gone. There will be no getting him back."

"I understand."

A pause.

"You will want later to change your mind, and you will be able to do nothing."

"I will not change my mind."

"But this is not so easy to arrange. *Pour la crémation,* one must first obtain permission of the relatives."

"He has no relatives in France."

"Then we must arrange for permission from his American relatives."

"I am legally authorized to act in his stead."

"This may be true in America, but you are not in America. You are in France. You are not a relative. They will have precedence."

"His parents are aged. They are eager for me to discharge these matters. I have spoken with them. They, too, wish for their son to be cremated."

"This may be true, but we must receive proof in writing."

"In writing?"

"*Oui, monsieur.* Notarized. In French. *S'il vous plaît.*"

"But of course." (*Pas de problème,* I thought, for his German-speaking, ninety-year-old father, many thousand miles and nine time zones distant.)

"*Je suis désolé,* but these are regulations."

"I will obtain the necessary permissions. In French. You will arrange the cremation."

The shoulders rose, the eyebrows knitted, the lower lip thrust out. "But this is not so easy to arrange. One must make an appointment at the crematorium."

"Any one you choose will do."

"Choose?"

"I am not particular as to where the cremation is accomplished."

"But there is no choice. There is only one."

"In all Paris? One crematorium?"

"*Oui, monsieur. Nous sommes un pays catholique.*" ("We are a Catholic country.")

A pause.

"Then telephone that one. Monsieur Rose and I are alone here, we want no ceremony in this matter."

"But this is not so easy to arrange. There is only space for one—individual."

"Then please check for the first available space."

The shoulders raised, the lips pursed.

"But this is not so easy to arrange. This is Thursday, the crematorium is closed Saturday and Sunday. There is the paperwork to accomplish."

"Of course. You will see when there is a space open, and we will discuss matters from there."

A phone call, some friendly conversation (a flurry of intimate *tus* and *tois*), a consultation of calendars. Monsieur Grenier hung up, folding his hands in satisfaction.

"We have reserved Thursday three weeks from today."

"*C'est pas possible.*"

"But, Monsieur Johnson, you need not attend Monsieur Rose. We will arrange the service for you, you may fly back to America, we will send the ashes later. This happens all the time."

"But we—I do not want a service."

"You must have a service."

"*C'est pas possible.* You will check again. I will pay more, if that is of use." (The rush premium, I thought.)

The shoulders dropped. Another phone conversation.

"We may arrange two weeks from next Monday."

"*C'est pas possible.*"

"*Mais,* Monsieur Johnson, you will want to rent a room at the crematorium, to bring proper clothing for Monsieur Rose. The service must be arranged, this requires time as well."

"There will be no service."

"There must be a service."

"We will have the service in California."

"But what of the family, the friends?"

"There is no family. There are no friends. There is only me. I have no need for a service here. We will do this in California."

"But there is the *enlevé*. Surely you will want to view Monsieur Rose again."

A pause.

"Monsieur Grenier. Monsieur Rose and I are from California. As you may have heard, these matters are accomplished considerably more informally in California. I have made my farewells to Monsieur Rose. There will be no proper clothing. There will be no *enlevé*. There will be no service here in France."

"Flowers, for Monsieur Rose?"

"There will be no flowers."

A pause. He seemed stunned by the callousness of Americans, or perhaps by my refusal to spend money, but in the face of my obduracy he placed another call. "*Il n'a pas de famille,*" he said into the phone. ("He has no family.") "*Il était célibataire.*" ("He was single.")

He hung up, turned to me with an air of triumph.

"We have Friday, *une huitaine.*" ("A week from Friday.")

In despair, I spread my hands, dropped my jaw, lifted my shoulders: I became, for this moment, French.

"*Monsieur Grenier. On veut seulement quitter Paris.*" ("One wants only to leave Paris.")

Monsieur Grenier was not defeated—he would win this war, and I would pay dearly in reparations—but this battle, at least, he had lost. Because I had convinced him? Because he would lose a sizable commission if I went elsewhere? It hardly mattered; for whatever reason, a flicker of compassion crossed his smooth, young face. In years to come he might learn to suppress this weakness, but now he took up the phone again, this time for a conversation conducted very much sotto voce.

He turned to me a final time, not triumphant but resigned. "We have eleven forty-five A.M. Monday. You may receive the ashes from me on Tuesday. You understand that it cannot be done any faster than this."

"I understand, and I thank you for your help."

"*Alors.* You will bring a suit for Monsieur Rose."

"You may use the clothes that he wore to the hospital."

"But we have no suit jacket, only a sweater. When you see him for the last time, Monday morning, you will want him dressed in something more formal than a sweater."

"I do *not* want to see him Monday morning."

A pause.

"You will not see him Monday morning."

"I would, however, like to know the time of cremation, so that I may be at the crematorium."

"But you have no need to be present at the crematorium!"

"I *want* to be present at the crematorium. I would like to arrange my own small ceremony at the moment of his—*la crémation.*"

"Ah! So you will want a service!"

We finished our conversation. Monsieur Grenier produced some thick documents in an official French that I could not decipher with several days and a dictionary. These he pushed across the desk for me to sign. His silk sleeve rasped delicately against the desktop. It was a hot day in October, the hospital was not airconditioned, the room was still as death itself, and on that hot, stale air rode a scent I knew, I recognized, as evocative as the taste of Proust's madeleine dipped in tea; the scent of the cologne that Larry had forgone for me: Vetiver.

The next day, I visited the office of Dr. K., in the fashionable 16th Arrondissement. I had slept only fitfully since my arrival in Europe days earlier, and stress and grief were taking their toll. Walking the

Champs-Elysées to the airline ticket office to cancel Larry's seat, I'd begun to see double (two obelisks in the Place de la Concorde, two Arcs de Triomphe). I called Dr. K. because he'd been one of Larry's doctors at the American Hospital; he was the only doctor in Paris whom I knew.

A crystal chandelier hung from the ceiling, which was high enough to accommodate full-scale muraled walls. The furniture I guessed to be Louis XV, or a good imitation—the son's slightly sterner, slightly more austere version of the Sun King's extravagant baroque. Dr. K.'s walls were lined with books—medical texts, of course, but in addition whole shelves of classics of French literature, including an aged edition of Diderot's *Encyclopédie*.

Dr. K. entered. He was a dark, middle-aged man with thinning, close-cropped hair and a self-assured carriage. I found the presence of all that art not intimidating but comforting—evidence of some concern for the soul as well as the body, and already I suspected that my symptoms' causes were more than purely physiological. From habit and curiosity I sneaked a glance—he wore no wedding ring.

Accustomed to time-pressured American doctors, I began unbuttoning my shirt. He held up his hand. "*Un moment,*" he said, indicating a chair in which I should sit.

"*Vous lisez Monsieur Proust. Et votre ami—il était en train de lire Monsieur Flaubert.*" ("You are reading Monsieur Proust. And your friend—he was in the middle of reading Monsieur Flaubert.") When I'd checked Larry into the hospital, I'd assumed he'd have a lengthy stay, and I'd left behind the books we'd been reading separately during the trip. I'd not given them a thought, but on one of his late-night rounds Dr. K. had taken the time to look and register our reading choices. Now he launched into a discussion of French and American literature. When I mentioned that I was a writer, his face brightened visibly. He asked after my writing. For some minutes we discussed my work with the *New York Times*.

As with Monsieur Grenier, Dr. K. and I spoke in the politest of terms, seldom venturing out of the conditionals and subjunctives used to express reserve, *politesse*. Almost a half hour passed before he directed me to a medieval Japanese screen discreetly unfolded in one corner. If you would be so kind, he said. If you would not object. You may keep your underwear.

Undressing behind the screen, I considered how the act of removing one's clothes was more private than being unclothed. I considered that I was undergoing an examination different from what I had ever encountered at the hands of an American doctor.

Dr. K. conducted the tests I expected—"*S'il vous plaît, ouvrez la bouche.*" ("If you please, might you open your mouth?")—as well as several whose origins lay closer to acupressure or Eastern medicine. In the politest of tenses he requested my permission to conduct an examination of my prostate. Afterward he directed me to put my clothes on behind the screen. He returned to his desk, where I joined him.

"You may have heard of those who are trying to protect and preserve the French tongue. I am among those. Where a French word exists, I prefer to use it even if the *franglais* version is more common." *Franglais* he said with a contempt I'd reserve for the torturers of small furry animals. "You are suffering from what is commonly called *le stress,* though I will prefer to call it by a French name—*l'agression.*"

I don't much care what it's *called,* I thought. I just want it *over*. It would be some while before I understood that I was in the midst of a process that would require its own time, a process as organic as the growth of a tree and nearly as slow. Death had planted the seed of grief in my heart, which must and would gestate at its own pace, independent of my will.

Dr. K. detailed the symptoms of *le stress/l'agression:* blurry vision, headaches, sleeplessness. He discharged me with an admonition to take care of myself; contrary to the reputation of European doctors, he did not prescribe sleeping pills, which I could very much have used.

As I stood to leave, he rose to shake my hand—a French shake, the hand pumped exactly once, no more. "Permit me to praise your French, which is admirable." For a moment I thought I'd misunderstood. I could not imagine anyone complimenting my French. "You have a superb accent, an excellent vocabulary," he said. "I have rare occasion to say that to any foreigner, and very seldom to an American. You must have had excellent professors."

And so it was Monday, the day of Larry's cremation. I rose early and went into Paris alone; Larry's friend with whom we'd been staying, who was himself HIV-positive and growing ill, could not bear to accompany me to my informal memorial service.

I arrived at Galeries Lafayette shortly after it opened and bought two champagne flutes. "Might I have them washed?" I asked the salesgirl. "I'll be using them immediately." Puzzled, amused, nonetheless she complied. I bought a bottle of Veuve Clicquot and took the metro to the columbarium, to our journey's most fitting end: The single crematorium in Paris is in the columbarium at Cimetière du Père Lachaise, burial place of all those people whom we had read, loved, taught, listened to, whose tombs we'd visited together.

It was, of course, a lovely day—France would not fail us here. I arrived early, climbing the long sloping alleys that lead past the jumbled, cheek-by-jowl tombs. The horse chestnuts overhead were not the autumn colors of America—this was *douce France,* whose mild winters do not bring about New England's bursts of color. But seared-brown leaves were falling as I climbed, a slow and gentle rain of leaves that slackened or burst forth in collusion with the wind.

When Larry and I had first discussed our third trip to France, I argued for autumn for a number of reasons. I thought of my first experience in Europe, as a college student living in Tours in the autumn and winter of 1972–73. I thought of the tourists, or more accurately the lack of them. And I thought more than anything of that certain slant of light, so far north on the globe; the light of Fragonard and Monet, unearthly light to eyes used to the harsher, more vertical light of North America. At the time of these discussions, there was no doubt of the outcome of these matters, of Larry's death, and this time of year seemed right: this literal autumn in Europe for Larry, whose favorite place had been Paris; the autumn of the time we had been given.

And so here I was, walking under the shedding chestnuts, the roar of Paris fading, a little, as I walked deeper into the cemetery. I passed the Mur des Fédérés, site of the last stand of the Paris Commune, whose members lay buried here in a mass grave. I passed the monument to the French Jews deported, with French collaboration, to Nazi concentration camps. I passed by Colette and Maria Callas and Jim Morrison, Oscar Wilde and Apollinaire and Gertrude Stein, finally to reach Marcel Proust, whom I had chosen to read on this journey, on whose polished black gravestone, adjacent to the columbarium, Larry and I had once eaten lunch. I opened our champagne, poured us each a glass, and took up my book. At eleven forty-five I began to read aloud the twenty-fourth and last book of the *Odyssey*.

Here Homer tells of the end of Odysseus' journey, in a chapter that the Fitzgerald translation entitles "Farewell, Warriors." I smelled the briefest scent of burning wool, as the heavy sweater Larry had worn to the hospital, my gift to him on his fortieth birthday, began to burn.

The next afternoon I visited for the last time the offices of Monsieur Grenier. He brought forth the cremation urn and commented on its handsomeness, a leading comment I ignored. He handed me a sheaf of papers, bound with a scarlet ribbon run through a grommet in the upper-left-hand corner and sealed in scarlet wax with the biggest and most officious of impressions, this from the U.S. consulate. "You must be very careful with these," he warned. "If the seal is broken, the papers are invalidated, and we must start again from the beginning." A fat check disbursed, and I was on the street.

It was 5:30 P.M. in Neuilly. The rush-hour traffic was building, both the metro and the suburban train lines were on strike, there wasn't a taxi within blocks. And what would be the point, to find a taxi only to sit in gridlocked traffic? I carried in one hand a bag I'd brought to transport the urn, but which had turned out to be too small. In my other hand I carried an overcoat and umbrella (there was a threat of rain) and the box containing the urn. With my arm I clutched to my chest the precious papers bound in the flimsiest of French envelopes, no more than the thinnest scrap of paper between the crowds of Paris and the magic red seal, the breaking of which would plunge us both, myself and what was left of Larry, back into bureaucratic hell.

I fought my way onto the metro, amid glares and grumbling from the passengers, directed at this big-boned American stupid enough to carry baggage onto the subway at rush hour. At Châtelet ("world's largest subway station," the honorific came floating back to mind from the *Guide Michelin*) I descended, to face what might fairly be called a howling mob. No suburban-line trains were running between Châtelet and Gare du Nord, the only functioning suburban station. On the single metro line running to Gare du Nord, trains were running once every half hour.

I waited through two packed trains, then I returned to the street.

And I saw then the sweater store nearby, where a few days before Larry had tried to buy me the store's most expensive sweater; and I, having learned so little from life in more than three years, in nearly thirty-seven years, said, no, no, it's too expensive, we'll come back later. And now it was later, and we were back.

I entered the store. The sweater was on display now, a lovely Irish sweater that was, in fact, too expensive—Larry and his eye for the best! "You were in here last week," the high-cheekboned salesgirl said breezily. "You and your friend, who spoke such excellent French. Where is he?"

"Oh, he's here." She gave me a puzzled look. I bought the sweater.

So now I had the sweater, the umbrella, the overcoat, the bag for the urn that was too small to hold the urn, the urn itself in its box, the magic papers whose seal must be protected at all costs.

The salesclerk studied me carefully. "*Il y a une grève*," she said tentatively ("There's a strike")—not wanting to lose a sale, but concerned for this ignorant American's welfare.

I nodded.

"*Vous êtes trop chargé.*" ("You're carrying too much.")

I nodded and plunged into the city.

And then I was back in the English-speaking world. Arriving at Los Angeles International, carrying Larry's ashes in a nicely designed traveling box, I thought that maybe all this had happened in some parallel universe, that someday, in another life, I would be able to understand and absorb and comprehend it all; but waiting for our—*my* luggage to emerge from the baggage chute, it was impossible not to imagine that were I to stand here long enough, he would emerge from around a corner, grinning at the sly joke he'd played on us all.

The chute spat out its baggage. My battered suitcase arrived forlorn and alone—I'd disposed of Larry's suitcases in France, since they'd held mostly drugs, IV tubing, needles, and medical paraphernalia I saw no point in carting home. My southern California sisters greeted me, and as I hauled my bag to their car, I thought of journeys' ends. Orpheus and Eurydice: What had I done wrong? At one point did I violate some unspoken rule, turn and look back and so lose my love? *Five minutes,* I thought; *is this so much to ask?* That he might sit with me for five minutes, not so that I might say anything—we'd said all that needed to be said—but that I might see him whole and alive and home.

Except, I reminded myself, *he's already home, as home as it's possible to be.*

In the greatness of their grief Kathy and Fred did not at first want a memorial service, but I insisted—raised in a small town, I could not imagine a man's passing without some collective celebration of his life. They arranged a service for the day after my return. They'd never been regulars at temple, and the one rabbi they knew was out of town, so they were forced to locate a stranger, a rabbi who was kindly and intelligent but who faced the demands of speaking eloquently about a man he'd never known. I'd realized in advance the impossibility of his task, and so I gave over my long, sleepless flight from France to composing a eulogy. This was my task, I decided, to set my grief aside and to offer his parents comfort, and if that later caught up with me, this was the necessary price of being younger and stronger, of being his partner.

The service was held at Hollywood Park Cemetery, which as a burial place has shared both the meteoric rise and the crash of Hollywood itself. The neighboring streets were filled with auto repair shops, pawnbrokers, drug dealers. The cemetery staff themselves went about this business of appearances dressed in the shabbiest of cast-off clothes. The vastly overweight office manager insisted on officiating at Larry's service, where she appeared in a turquoise-flowered rayon muumuu, a screaming siren amid the grief and trouble of this small family.

The rabbi spoke the kaddish, then asked me to speak about Larry. I spoke of the circle of life and death, of our need to come together to remind us in our grief that this is the way it has always been, this is the way it must be, this is the way it should be. I refused to speak of sadness. Instead I spoke of that last journey to France, a place Larry had loved so much, where he'd gone with me, with whom he was in love. I spoke of his insistence on his good luck, and my foot-dragging education into the truth of what he said. I told the story of our evening in the courtyard of the Picasso Museum, of our last drive together through the beauty of the Loire.

To die in happiness, loved and in love—this is no small miracle, a gift we cannot question but can only accept, in gratefulness and humility.

I'd brought a passage from the writing of another great Jew, like Kathy and Fred a gift to America from war-torn Europe, and I ended by reading it. In a letter to the widow of his colleague and mentor Michaelangelo Besso, Albert Einstein wrote, "So once again he has gone before me a little. That doesn't matter very much. For those of us who believe in physics, this distinction between past, present, and future is an illusion, however tenacious."

So we left his ashes in Hollywood Park. If a man is measured by the company he keeps, Larry measures up; cremated among the pillars of Western European culture, Larry has his ashes stored in the company of Charlie Chaplin, Cecil B. De Mille, D. W. Griffith, Rudolph Valentino, Eleanor Powell, John Huston. From the monument to Abelard and Héloise in Père Lachaise to the monument to Cupid and Psyche in Hollywood Park—he was, finally, a Californian, and one could wish for his sake only that Lucille Ball was buried somewhere nearby.

We held the San Francisco service at a Jewish memorial chapel, where the cantor whom Larry and I had heard at Michael's service the year before kindly returned to sing kaddish. Well over a hundred people came, including thirty or forty of Larry's students, former and current, from Berkeley High.

There I took the chance to thank Kathy and Fred, who had never questioned my judgment or decisions—in the days following Larry's death, when an understandable response might have been anger or criticism, they had offered only unconditional love and support.

Among the students attending were the girls who'd written him mash notes; now young women, they'd returned from college for this service, one flying in from Los Angeles. The day I began cleaning out Larry's office, I'd found their sympathy note to Larry taped to the wall above his desk. On the inside flap of his memorial announcement I reprinted the last four lines of the Shakespeare sonnet they'd quoted.

> In others' works thou dost but mend the style,
> And arts with thy sweet graces gracèd be;
> But thou art all my art, and dost advance
> As high as learning my rude ignorance.

Now I read the complete sonnet. "We know almost nothing of the person to whom Shakespeare addressed his sonnets—including his love sonnets—except that he was a man," I said. "I think this is a sonnet about the relationship between teaching and love, how one may follow from the other, how teaching informed by love and love informed by teaching enable each to achieve its highest expression.

"Without love, Shakespeare tells us, teaching is superficial repair work—'In others' works thou dost but mend the style.' It's love which transforms both teacher and student: 'But thou art all my art, and dost advance / As high as learning my rude ignorance.' I want to thank the students who sent the sonnet to Larry—who enabled me and all of us to learn from it."

I asked other students to tell stories they might have of Mr. Rose. They were reluctant to speak at first, until a young man with rings in his nose and lower lip stood. "The first time we read Shakespeare, Mr. Rose asked us to write a paper, and I wrote that I thought Shakespeare was full of shit, nothing else," he said.

Oh, brave new world, I thought amid my grief, *when kids invoke four-letter words in their eulogies.*

"I thought that would shake him up for sure, and I was in that place, you know, where I wanted to shake the teacher up. But he sat me down with the paper and said, 'Explain to me why Shakespeare is full of shit, and then we'll see if you can get that across in writing.' And he made me stay after, like, three or four times and explain every time what I hated about each of the poems we read, and then he made me go home and write that down, and after a while I explained enough about them that I kind of forgot that I didn't like them and decided they were pretty good."

Another student stood. "He made me go a month without grades on my papers, only his comments, until I started reading the comments and taking them to heart."

"He made us do this exercise," another said, "where he took us out to Telegraph Avenue and made us write about what we saw until we thought it was good enough to convince somebody who'd never been there what it looked like and what we thought of it. It was the first time in my life I really understood what writing was about—trying to get something real across to another, faraway person through this incredibly abstract medium. It was the first time in my life I wrote something I thought was really good."

They were raising hands left and right now, telling stories Larry had never told me (who was this man I'd loved and lived with?). Finally I had to cut them off so that the cantor might rise to sing. An elderly man with a clear, pure tenor, his voice held the kaddish's blend of sorrow and comfort, mourning and peace.

To close the service I quoted a passage from the writing of another great Jew, Issac Bashevis Singer, writing in his novel *Shosha:*

> How is it possible, after all, that someone should simply vanish? How can someone who lived, loved, and wrangled with God and with himself just disappear? I don't know how and in what sense but they're here. Since time is an illusion, why shouldn't everything remain?

On a discouraging night not long after Larry's death, I wrote my next-older sister, who had herself helped a lover through his death from leukemia. "Tell me, O older and wiser sister," I wrote, "how long will this grief last?" Older and wiser, she wrote back: "Grief is never over. The time will come when you control your grief rather than the other way around. You'll draw upon those memories when you need and want them, rather than having them show up uninvited. But your grief will never go away, which is the way it should be. It and Larry are part of who you are."

I am a man of few landscapes. Twice I have moved away from San Francisco and twice I have returned, not because of its tolerance or its fog (though I value both) but because I wanted to be near old friends. Looking back, I see that I was trying to re-create in a big city something like the blood family among whom I'd been raised, where on each walk to school I passed two centuries of my genealogy lying in the churchyard.

Now I am not much past forty, but of those whom I returned to be near, many are dead. Even in this city of small neighborhoods, many of the men from whom I learned to respect myself will not unexpectedly round the corner some bright autumn afternoon; I run little risk of the pleasant dangers of random encounters with my past, except in the recesses of my heart.

These days I visit with those dead men, my friends and lovers, though (as my sister predicted) on my terms, not theirs. The imperative to live presses its demands and I comply. Though I commonly have vivid dreams, I seldom dream of them; I never dream of Larry, a fact that saddens me. Maybe after I finish this book, I tell myself, that will change.

But writing is a contemplative profession. In exchange for solitude and various financial and psychological insecurities, I am given the luxury to daydream, and when in midafternoon I release my mind to wander, this is the place it often chooses to visit:

A large grassy bank cradled in the oxbow bend of a river flowing through a deciduous place, curving past a hardwood forest of oak and hickory and walnut—the landscape of my childhood asserts itself, though here and there a redwood pierces this temperate forest's profile and the stream runs clear and gravel-bottomed; I have lived many years in northern California. Mitt-leaved sassafras in the undergrowth—the air smells of cinnamon as I push through. The riverbank is populated with men, men who have loved me and whom I've loved, and men whom I've wanted to love: men I wanted to date but hadn't the courage or time to ask; men who rejected me, men whom I rejected; men I saw only once, on an airplane, in a bar, on a crowded bus, on a nearly empty beach, in a foreign land, in a classroom, in a church. Many of them are surely ill or dead, but they are all here, sons of the mothers of the world, alive and full of joy on the grassy bank of my heart, here at the cusp of their lives and somewhere in their midst sits Larry, my Larry. Young enough still to be beautiful, old enough to know the meaning of the coolness beneath the sun's warmth; old enough to know that every shadow promises night; old enough to know death. I cross that river to join them. We are gathered by a river where we have knowledge of time outside of time, of death without death, and there on the grassy green bank of my east-west heart, in the endless low-slanting sun, we give ourselves over to making memory and remembering.

Lucky Fellows

i

In writing of my journeys I am done with talk of death except as it is a part of life, one side of a sphere whose roundness would otherwise be incomplete. In a letter to his protégé Émile Bernard, van Gogh wrote, "The earth had been thought to be flat . . . science has proved that the earth is round . . . they persist nowadays in believing that life is flat and runs from birth to death. However, life, too, is probably round."

Show me the beginning and ending of a sphere; then I will show you the beginning and ending of a life.

ii

Not long after Larry's death, a friend took me out to dinner. We sat and ordered drinks, then she took my hand and said, "Tell me the whole story."

I looked at her blankly. We'd spoken several times since I'd returned from France, she'd been at his memorial service, at one point or another she'd heard the facts. What else was there to tell?

"I want to hear the *whole* story," she said. "From beginning to end." For the next several hours she listened while I poured out the whole story, and so took my first steps toward becoming whole myself.

iii

For the Christmas holidays following Larry's death, I returned to my childhood home in Kentucky. There my mother had bravely placed Larry's photograph and memorial announcement in a prominent spot, where everyone might see it and its request for donations to AIDS charities. At the same time, no one in the family asked after the story of his death or how I was doing or expressed sympathy. The contradiction hung over Christmas like emotional smog. My family wanted to be supportive but couldn't bring themselves to break the silence surrounding so many taboos: my love for men, AIDS, death. Sunk in grief, I waited for them to speak.

Until 3 A.M. on the night before I was to return to San Francisco, one of those white nights between Christmas and New Year's when several of my nephews, all in their twenties, were sitting around the kitchen table putting a larger dent in the holiday liquor supply than their parents (my older brothers and sisters) might have liked. I'd tried twice to go to bed, to be kept awake by the knowledge that only the living can do justice to the memory of the dead. To acquiesce in silence would be to deny and so to betray their memories, their lives, their loves.

I returned to the kitchen a third time. I opened my mouth: nothing. I hovered at the edge of the conversation, a tongue-tied Ghost of Christmas to Come, until my next-oldest sister asked bluntly, "What's on *your* mind?"

Her question gave me courage, or at least put me on the spot, and I answered in a breathless torrent of words: "I'm filled with bitterness and rage that no one will acknowledge that Larry was my lover and that he died of AIDS, and I'm here to give the first annual AIDS prevention speech."

Silence. But: rapt attention.

The extent of my hip, college-educated nephews' curiosity turned out to be exceeded only by the magnitude of their ignorance. Their questions ranged from the ludicrous to the touchingly explicit. One understood HIV as more or less omnipresent, like common cold viruses, but precipitated from thin air by the heat of sex. My older, college-educated sister insisted that she knew a woman who had contracted the virus from sitting in a hot tub with an infected man.

As we talked, I realized that I was the first person from the preceding generation to speak with my nephews about sex without passing judgment—the first to offer them information with no strings attached. This was far deeper water than I had anticipated, but once off the diving board I had no choice but to swim. If I'd thought before speaking, it would have been to hope that I could talk about HIV without discussing, well, *details*. My nephews were too starved for information to allow that. "What about kissing?" one asked.

"I kissed an HIV-positive man for more than three years and I still test negative," I said.

"What about when you're going at it with a girl and she gets all juicy and you get that on your fingers?" another asked, and the question implied its own abyss.

"If you're ignorant of your partner's history, and you have reason to believe she or he may be at risk, you might consider latex gloves." A collective grimace. I fixed my eyes on some imaginary point above and beyond my nephews' heads. "They're not so bad. Larry and I had great, messy sex. Often."

"You're blushing." This from my helpful sister.

"These were our rules." Was I saying this? To my nephews? "We always used condoms. He never came inside me. I never came inside him."

"But wasn't that dangerous?" one asked.

"Life is dangerous!" I cried. "Driving a car is riskier than having safe sex, and you never give driving a second thought. What you do is educate yourself to the risks and then act to minimize them. Have as many partners as you can be careful and considerate with, if that's what you want. Careful *and* considerate. But if nothing else, be careful. If you do needle drugs—"

"Oh, no, we'd never be that stupid," they chorused.

"I'm glad to hear it, but I'm not asking if you'd be that stupid. That's a different talk. I'm telling you how to take care of your-selves."

The next day I rode to the airport with one of my brothers. When I told him I'd delivered the first annual AIDS prevention speech to his sons, he was pleased. Then he told me that as part of his job he delivered AIDS awareness talks to his fellow employees. *So why haven't you delivered one to your kids?* I thought, but I said nothing, even though my own experience taught me the answer. Once again my courage evaporated in the face of the great silence.

My nephews' questions might have been naïve, but I left Kentucky wondering why I had kept silent for so long among my family. I was the one who had known about HIV for years, after all. I had watched friends and a lover grow sick and die, and yet I had said nothing on my visits among those who have no ready access to information, for whom my speaking might make the greatest dif-ference. Why had I found it so hard to act among my family—to speak out among people whom I love?

An easy explanation leapt to mind, one that let me off the hook. It was because these were matters of the heart. The emotions that brought me to care in the first place stifled my tongue.

Well, partly. But I was also trying to preserve my most cher-ished illusion—that I'm in control. As a gay teenager forced to conceal my desire behind a façade of indifference or lies, I learned the importance of sustaining the illusion of control. But many peo-ple and most men learn some variation of the same illusion, for our culture rewards nothing so much as stoic indifference.

Both sex and death mock that pleasant illusion. To address them at the same time, as talking about HIV required, meant giving up that illusion, in exchange for a head-on encounter with the mystery that inhabits the heart of being.

Thinking about these matters on the plane back to San Francisco, I came to understand that something more than HIV education was behind my Christmas speech to my middle-American nephews. I wanted them to understand HIV and its means of transmission, but I also wanted to get them to thinking about the cheerful diversity of sexuality and the miraculously infinite ways of being in the world. I wanted to get them thinking about the enormity of the gap between the tidy, manageable world we pretend to and advertise and the great, sprawling, mysterious world in which we really live. I hoped to bring them to make their own connections between even the most casual sex and some kind of love: caring enough for one's partner and oneself to establish and respect limits.

And I understood that I'd spoken out for my own well-being as much as for theirs. I needed to free myself of lies. I needed truth, which, I was discovering, was not to be accomplished in any single gesture but had to be lived out day by day, act by act.

I returned to Kentucky for the following Christmas, but this time my nephews drove me to the airport. I seized the chance to deliver the second annual AIDS prevention speech, but what was important was less the passing on of information than the conversation that followed. During the hour-plus drive, we talked about genealogy, family history, their father's divorce—how it affected their lives, why he had found it so difficult to talk to them and they to him. I cautioned them against holding the previous generation to unrealistic standards. "Love is about forgiveness," I said—an acknowledgment that the beloved is human and fallible, and a decision to love him or her despite or maybe because of that knowledge.

As we talked, I realized that because I'd spoken out—because I took a risk, because I made myself vulnerable—they'd rewarded me with their trust. I had become for them another, different kind of father: a comrade and repository of family history; a bridge between them and their biological father.

My brother had given his children love of a duration and depth I could only admire and learn from, but my own love had its necessary place. I was younger; I hadn't the inevitable and necessary burden of being a father; I could say things to his children that he might never find his way to saying. In this way maybe all of us— grandparents, friends, aunts, uncles, cousins, lovers, parents— could find our ways to our particular roles in defining what family is about. Brought together by a chance alignment of stars, histories, and genes, we could act to build families based on love.

iv

Across the first year after Larry's death, I became friends with Mark, a man whose lover of a decade had slowly been dying for more than two years. On Mark's birthday, a year or so after we met, I called and offered him these options: coming to my place for lunch; going out for lunch, my treat. He chose coming to my place, which on that particular Friday carried some sad and delicious possibility of sex.

I was cheered by the prospect of leaving off work to spend a Friday afternoon with drop-dead-handsome Mark. In conversation we never talked of our lovers, dying or dead, but we'd established that it had been at least two years since Mark had made love and nearly as long for me—in the last months before Larry's death, he'd grown too weak to make love. In our mutual caretaking Mark and I had carefully avoided talk of the future, content with holding another person's commiserating hand (the hand-holding had been mostly metaphorical, Mark being caught up in that man thing, and after two years of living-with-dying very much into guarding his heart).

So I went out and bought birthday candles and a couple of

chocolate cupcakes and a book for a gift, and came home and wrapped the book and set the table and stuck the candles in the cupcakes and took a shower.

And I was climbing from the shower and searching for a clean pair of Calvin Klein's when the phone rang and it was Mark, saying that his lover had just gotten the results from his latest test and it was *Pneumocystis* again, and his doctor had exhausted all the drugs used to treat it and didn't know what he could do, and Mark wanted to spend the afternoon consoling his lover at this grim turn of events. I made some comments I hoped were supportive, then I hung up and got dressed (the ragged old Fruit of the Loom's would do) and ate my bowl of soup and one of the chocolate cupcakes and resigned myself to resuming work.

But as I sat to my work, the phone rang again, and it was Mark, saying that the doctor had called back to say he'd heard about an experimental drug that killed only 10 percent of the people who took it, and he'd send it over to start Mark's lover on it right away. And since for the moment Mark's lover was feeling okay and since it was Mark's birthday, maybe he would come over for lunch. So he did in fact come over and I fed him soup and lit the candles on the remaining cupcake. He carved it in two and gave me half, and in his gesture I understood what we both wanted: that short triumph over fate, over time and memory and history, that desire may bring at its best.

And on that day it turned out to be very much at its best. The old confusion of love and sex and death carried (safely) to the limit; a modest act of defiance, a declaration of life, thumbing our noses in the face of the beast.

Then I took Mark's hand and he took it back and pulled on his clothes and went home to his dying lover.

V

My first date, a year and a half after Larry's death: I'd met a land-scape architect who lived in the East Bay, whom I invited to accompany me to the theater. I crossed the Bay Bridge to Oakland, where a full moon rose above hills burned clear in the firestorm that swept through in autumn 1991. Tom, my date, was a nice-looking guy with a steady paycheck—every writer's fantasy. When he told me he was *reading a novel,* I was impressed and for a long minute bedeviled by stupid, involuntary fantasies of a partner, someone to fill this void left by Larry's death.

And then through the evening, no mention of his long-term plans; none of the casual references to the future that pepper our conversations and of which we're not even aware, and all the while that dark knowledge growing larger and more unavoidable.

Then it was after the play, he was driving me back to my car, and the air was charged with possibility. Never good at leaving well enough alone, I broke the silence by asking what he was reading, which turned out to be Stephen King, but that was okay, I didn't hold it against him. "I'm an Anne Rice fan myself," I said—a small enough lie for a first date. From vampire novels I made an easy conversational leap to complaining about the mess of blackberry briers my landlord called a yard.

"What you need is a landscape architect," Tom said.

"We'll both be old men before I can afford you," I said.

An awkward pause.

Tom cleared his throat. "There's something you ought to know," he said, but I'd figured it out already, I didn't need to be told and I didn't want to hear it. I covered his free hand with mine. "Next date," I said.

And then I was homeward bound after a chaste peck on the

cheek from Tom, but the heart's landscape wanted company and so I drove not west across the Bay Bridge but east into the burned and blackened Oakland hills. There I parked on some fire-ravaged lane and stepped from the car. No houses or trees were left to block the view—the long cantilevered bridge, the dark mass of Yerba Buena Island rising from the bay's black mirror, the city's glittering towers. The full moon painted the ash-covered earth in whiteface.

I walked up a driveway leading past the mangled remains of a mailbox to a rectangular hole—the foundation of someone's life. I looked across the bay to San Francisco and in bitterness I thought, *The best gays and lesbians can hope for from mainstream religion is to be left alone, but we all need somebody, the earth needs somebody in these tough times to hold up some light, to say, yes, death comes but it's part of the great cycle, how can we know love without knowing loss, there is joy in accepting the mystery in which we're immersed.* And I'd set out to learn these things, and a time had arrived when I could think, *Yes, that's right, I'm getting it.* And then someone like Tom appeared in my life and everything about his grace and beauty and infection said, *Find some joy here, dolt.*

I thought about all this and all I could manage was a sad smile, a reaction I couldn't explain then and can't explain now, but the next day when I mentioned it to a straight friend from the suburbs, he looked at me as if I were losing my mind. And maybe I was; or was this just the difference between those inside the epidemic and those looking on? What had I been brought to? "The lucky fellow," Elie Wiesel wrote of the terrorist leader in *Dawn*. "At least he can cry. When a man weeps he knows that one day he will stop."

vi

I visited Bill, a friend whose lover had died a few months before Larry and who was himself HIV-positive. His disease had progressed rapidly since the last time I'd seen him, to the point where he'd been blinded by the same opportunistic infection I'd once feared would blind Larry.

I arrived just as Bill was sitting to an unhappily familiar routine—administering his daily IV treatment. His sister brought him the medical equipment, while I chose some music—Natalie Cole. Like Larry, Bill insisted on hooking up by himself the IV pump that delivered drugs to a catheter concealed under his shirt. But he couldn't see well enough to locate the catheter with the needle, and his sister came to help. She tried to hook up the needle and pricked her finger.

A moment of dreadful silence, in which we all thought about the plague, and how it's spread, and what a tragedy it would be if Bill's sister, who had come across the continent to care for her brother, were somehow to contract the disease in her caregiving.

I'd done this with Larry, I knew how the IV works; I knew that the needle with which she'd pricked herself was not the needle that fed into her brother's bloodstream but the needle that fit into his external catheter. The chances of her having infected herself from such a needle prick were virtually nonexistent—the needle with which she'd pricked herself had never been in direct contact with Bill's blood. But the horror of the possibility reared its head all the same. She hurried to the kitchen. Bill called after her to wash the wound with iodine. I rose to pick up some medical paraphernalia Bill's sister had dropped, only to get her blood on my hand. I stared at my hand.

We all pretended this wasn't happening, or if it was happening, that it really didn't matter. I dropped the bloodied paraphernalia in the trash can. The sister returned from washing her hands and shrugged with affected unconcern. "No big deal," she said.

I know how the disease can and can't be spread; I know the odds. But I'm a white, more-or-less prosperous American man, so used to the assumption of predictability and security that I don't even know I assume it. I'm a child of the Enlightenment, inheritor and purveyor of a culture that assumes that everything can or will be explained and controlled. I've surrounded myself with gadgets (flip a switch, push a button) that demonstrate how completely I control the world—such a comforting illusion. Then chance, circumstance, luck—call it what I want—enters my life in any of its infinite guises, and I'm thrown for a loop. I've been so oblivious to any reminder of life's nonstop tenuousness.

Bill got his catheter to drip correctly. Natalie Cole launched into "Unforgettable." We settled into a tinny, bright conversation.

vii

A few weeks later I told Bill's story to a friend, a reporter in France. He responded with a story of women refugees who have fled to Paris from the brutal civil wars of Bosnia. There they avoid the company of all but other Bosnian refugees because, one told him, they cannot bear to be in the presence of people who so casually assume their lives.

This, it seems to me, is what the wisest HIV-positive men have come to terms with, the terrible and transcendent gift that I might take from them if I have enough courage: As much as I, they're caught up in life's day-to-day details, but they carry with them always the most intimate consciousness of the preciousness of life.

"If we had a keen vision and feeling of all ordinary human life," wrote George Eliot, "it would be like hearing the grass grow and the squirrel's heart beat, and we should die of that roar which lies on the other side of silence. As it is, the quickest of us walk about well wadded with stupidity." For a little over three years Larry stripped away my wadding—an accurate enough description, I think, of the state of many gay men of my generation. I was shocked from complacency into an ongoing, moment-to-moment appreciation of what I'd been given.

To be spared complacency, or shocked from it—this is no small gift, however its price may be unbearably high. To live with that intensity is a brilliant thing—years after Larry's death, I'm still daunted by the courage it requires; but even now, years later, no day passes without some small reminder of how immeasurably poorer my life would have been had Larry not brought me to this sun-drenched place. To know at the same moment these very different places—to possess simultaneously both joy in love and life, and an acceptance of loss and death—surely this is the whole round picture of what it means to be alive.

In an after-dinner conversation, an HIV-positive friend spoke casually of a time "before my body was contaminated." Only after the deaths of so many friends do I comprehend the courage required for my friend to say this simple phrase. I am struggling to learn from that courage—lessons in how to live and how to die.

I am painfully aware of the privileged position from which I write. As an HIV-negative person, I have been spared; in the most crude and obvious way, I have been lucky. I want to make clear that I am not suggesting, God forbid, that the arrival of HIV was in any way good. I am saying that those who transcend bitterness are our true teachers. Whether their particular trauma makes headlines is irrelevant—the whole fate of humanity expresses itself in each of our deaths. What is of consequence is how we live—how we arrive at our deaths; what we make with what we have been given.

viii

Shortly after Larry died, I began phoning Kathy and Fred, not as frequently as Larry had once done, but for the same, brief chats. Now it was my friends' turn to scoff. "You phone them *twice a week?*" one asked.

I considered this a moment. "Is it so great a burden, to phone an elderly couple twice a week for two or three minutes?"

I began visiting them in Santa Monica, two or three times a year. Once I'd found the prospect of such visits impossible to contemplate, an intrusion on my time; now I looked forward to sharing my grief with the only people who felt it as or more deeply than I.

My visits to Fred and Kathy's settled into a pattern: Occasionally I'd arrange business in Los Angeles, and I'd drop by their Santa Monica bungalow. Or I'd fly down for special occasions, such as the celebration of Fred's ninetieth birthday, when for an evening he regained some part of the irrepressible charm that had once been his calling card.

On such a visit, almost two years after Larry's death, Kathy answered the door—a role that always before had been Fred's. I saw him behind her, trying to rise from the couch to greet me. He was dressed in a wrinkled shirt open at the throat and an old pair of worn pants; at midday he was unshaven, his silver hair springing up in a wild thatch. Seeing him this way, I understood for the first time how his meticulous dressing had been another layer of defense against his past. Seeing him so disheveled and unkempt, I knew that he was dying.

On that hellishly hot July day, Kathy and I took Fred on a round of doctors' appointments, to encounter at each office faces more opaque and evasive than those of their predecessors. Finally we brought him home, where I helped him through the heat and into the house. He was diagnosed with pancreatic cancer and given less than a month to live.

Across that month Kathy stood vigil day and night. Fred did not want to enter a hospital; very well, she would make it possible for him to stay at home, if only through her willpower. She resisted entreaties from her family and from me to move him to a facility where she would have some help in her caretaking. She lifted him in and out of bed, bathed him as best she could, administered morphine when his pain grew too great to bear. She was with him when he died, as he wished, at home and in their bed; this tiny woman with the strength of ten, whose gift has been to love two men, whose place has been to bury both.

ix

For the sixth or seventh year running I marched in San Francisco's annual AIDS candlelight memorial. While walking, I encountered a longtime acquaintance, a man who aspired to write, who took the occasion to tell me how my "sticking with it" had inspired him, how he'd taken me as a role model for his life. I was reminded how we touch the lives of people we hardly know, or know not at all, and of the responsibilities implied by that symbiosis—the best argument for virtue that I know.

By the time I write this, my friend will be dead, but on that particular evening we walked side by side, down Market Street from the Castro district to City Hall. There a minister read the names of his congregation who had died from AIDS and asked the crowd to shout out the names of friends and loved ones who had died.

All around me people were screaming their heads off, furious, but I didn't scream. To scream would be to risk sabotaging my house of cards, so laboriously reconstructed after Larry's death. Instead I whispered, "Salvador Franco. Fred Rosenberg. Michael Rubin. Bill Bradley. Steven Rosen. Michael O'Neal. Larry Rose . . ." Somewhere in the middle of this litany I realized that I was praying, and I continued my prayer long after the last shouts had echoed from the columns and dome of the great wedding cake of San Francisco's City Hall and lost themselves in the far reaches of the plaza. Last of all I spoke the name of a boy—too young to be called a man—from my hometown, population eight hundred, buried in the Kentucky hills. He returned from the city to die among his family, who embraced him and supported him until his death. I never knew him except from the whispered rumors that I hear when I return to my hometown for visits. In that culture of storytellers, no one speaks aloud his name, or the stories of his life. In that culture still in love with language, his family mourns him in silence.

I find this almost unbearably sad to consider—this confusion of sorrow with shame, this grieving in silence, where at his death a man simply vanishes, and those who have loved him at such cost to themselves have no choice but to collaborate in his disappearance.

Where does it go, all this energy of grief? What is the cost of cutting love from a heart?

This is what the ill and the dead have given me: an appreciation of the soul, an understanding of the spirit, how pure these words are, how absent from our culture, how great is our particular responsibility to restore them—as artists, as writers, as vessels for the stories of our dead.

As I have participated in the deaths of so many of my peers, I have come to believe passionately in the ways in which words—in this case the names and stories of our dead—have the power to invoke among us the presence of those who, as Orthodox Jews would have it, have traded the world of appearance for the world of truth. This is why remembering and speaking out are so important. Through remembering—through invoking the names and stories of those I have loved——I engage my most essentially human quality. Human beings are animals who remember and tell stories——as much as any other, this characteristic distinguishes us from our fellow creatures. The dead have given me an awareness of the mystery of life and death. I have a responsibility to remember them by living out that gift.

I think about all this; then I remember a story of someone or some place gone from my life and tell it to somebody else, and in the telling of that story take my proper and necessary place in the chain of being.

X

Not long after Larry and I moved in together: a summer evening when he was at his healthiest, and it was possible to believe that we would be given two or six or ten years together in the three-bedroom apartment with the great view and the aging cat. We were sitting on the deck not long before sunset, watching the fog peer over the hills. The moon, thinnest of Arabian crescents, was descending into the weird red cage of the radio tower that squats on Twin Peaks. Larry brought out the camera——he wanted to send his parents pictures of the view from the new apartment.

He took photos of the view, then we clowned for each other in front of the camera——more pictures for the overflowing box that now sits at one end of my desk. I waggled my fingers above my head and mugged for Larry, then it was his turn. He stuck his fingers in the corners of his mouth and eyes and pulled his face into a wacky grin, all squinty eyes and bared teeth, while in the background the slip of a moon tangled itself in the radio tower's webbing of cables and girders.

Afterward we wrapped ourselves in blankets and watched as the moon freed itself of the radio tower and sank into the fog. We talked a little about this and that—nothing important; end-of-the-day partner talk. I wasn't paying much attention. I was thinking about all kinds of pressing matters—what I was going to work on tomorrow and the impossible deadline I was facing and how was I going to make time for Larry amid all this work that was supposed to have been done yesterday, and somewhere in the middle of my thoughts he spoke up and said something like this: "Love is like a ripe peach. You take it when and where you find it, there's no point in letting it sit around. If you're lucky enough to come across it, you'd better enjoy it right then and there."

Later that summer, when he grew really, evidently, seriously ill, I thought, as little as possible but inevitably, of what would become of me after he died. I figured, of course, that a relatively young person who'd lost a great love would have a chance at such a love again—after all, that would be only fair. Then Larry died, and time and more time passed, and I came to understand how fairness has nothing to do with how and when love arrives; that I can be grateful for love only when and while it's happening, when it's quite literally in the hand.

xi

Surely we are all dealing with this, HIV-negative or HIV-positive, irrespective of our gender or sexualities: incorporating loss into life; substituting for the myth of control a reality that embraces light *and* dark, love *and* grief, life *and* death.

In the earliest years of the epidemic in San Francisco, this was the party line that we were all engaged to support: HIV-positive men would live forever, had as much claim as any of us on the myth of immortality. New drugs or new therapies, or old drugs

and old therapies, or crystals or visualization, or simply our ignorance of the long-term workings of the virus gave us the right to
this hope.

All this was true, except for one small problem: The emperor
had no clothes. The myth of immortality was just that, as much a
myth for the HIV-negative as the HIV-positive, as much a myth for
you as for me.

Before helping Larry die, I considered the myth that I would
live forever (when I considered it at all) as necessary insulation that
enabled me to carry on with daily life. Now that I have been
brought to understand how we all live continually in the presence
of death, insulation is not an option.

We are all survivors, after all, we are all mourners on this mor-
tal earth, who choose daily the measure of our participation (or
lack thereof) in the world's fate, which is to say its mortality,
which is to say its grief. It's just that HIV, with its extended incuba-
tion period, its prolonged illnesses, its often horrifying complications, its impact on close-knit neighborhoods and communities, is
forcing gay men of my generation to acknowledge what our life-
and youth-obsessed society prefers to deny.

"Write about the courage it takes to live in denial," a straight
friend urges me, meaning, I suppose, the willpower required to
live as if one has a long-term future when so many signs point to
the contrary. I think of David Weissman's short film *Song from an
Angel,* in which Rodney Price, founder of the 1970s theater troupe
Angels of Light, sings from his wheelchair, less than two weeks
before his death, an original song entitled "I've Got Less Time Than
You" ("If I look thinner / Take me to dinner / 'Cause I've got less
time than you, oh yeah / I've got less time than yo-oo-ou").

How is it possible to deny an illness for which one takes medication every four hours? The wisest people of my life, positive or
negative, are living not in denial but in acceptance, a state not of forgive and forget but of forgive and remember. This, it strikes me, is
the mourner's most difficult and necessary of tasks, the holding in

the heart of these contradictory imperatives: forgive and remember; accept and never shut up.

Grief is love's alter ego, after all, yin to its yang, the necessary other; like night, grief has its own dark beauty. How may we know light without knowledge of dark? How may we know love without sorrow? "The disorientation following such loss can be terrible, I know," Wendell Berry wrote me on learning of Larry's death. "But grief gives the full measure of love, and it is somehow reassuring to learn, even by suffering, how large and powerful love is."

xii

Enough time passes and I discover that I no longer measure time against how long it's been since Larry died.

My mother returns to visit San Francisco. We are driving north to Muir Woods to seek out the earliest spring wildflowers, which she has taught me to appreciate.

In our relationship I have always been in charge of raising emotional issues. Though she has known for many years that I'm gay, until Larry's death she found it difficult to speak to me of such matters, partly from fear of intruding past the wall I myself had maintained for so long, partly because (like all who were raised without such words) she has had to learn and grow comfortable with a new vocabulary to describe my life and her place in it ("my gay son," "his partner, who died of AIDS"). A country woman with little more than a high school education, she traveled very little until late in her life, but she has taught herself that new vocabulary. In part it is her experience learning it—in staying open to what her heart tells her is right and true—that has kept her young.

Now for the first time I can recall, she broaches the subject of my emotional life. She speaks in that lovely, circuitous, Southern narrative style—she begins by asking after Larry's mother, then after his family, then she reminisces briefly about his visit to Kentucky, then she talks of her visit to San Francisco in the summer before he died, when Larry drove up the coast to rescue us when my car battery died. After she has laid the groundwork by telling these stories, she takes up the heart of what she wants to say—the point of her remembering:

"I always thought of myself as tolerant and open-minded. I grew up with people who were gay, though of course back then we didn't use that word. I knew some people in our town were gay, everyone knew they were gay, but I didn't think much about that one way or another. Just live and let live, that's my way of being in the world. And then you told me you were gay, and I guess I'd suspected it all along, and I just prayed that you'd stay healthy and find yourself a place where you could be happy. I prayed for all that and I was glad to see you get yourself to San Francisco, to a place where you could live in peace and be yourself. I was happy about that, but it wasn't until I met you and Larry and spent time with the two of you together that I understood that two men could love each other in the same way as a man and a woman."

This speaking is the sacred thing, the gift from the dead to the living.

Of Larry's tightly bound family triangle, the mother endures.

I stay in touch with Kathy, who resists my gentle encouragement to form a life apart from her memories. From time to time she has sent me money, which for the most part I have accepted graciously, though occasionally my stubbornness asserts itself and we reenact uncomfortably familiar scenes in which I resist her generosity. She has accepted, I think, that I am not and cannot be a replacement for her son. For my part, I have accepted that there is no love worth the name without responsibility. We strive to find some kind of balance; more often than not we succeed.

I love better now, more wholly and completely, not because I have learned some exotic technique but because I know death.

More than four years since Larry's death, making love: My friend is stocky and tall, as tall as I but otherwise built unnervingly like Larry and with a shock of salt-and-pepper hair that is thicker even than Larry's was. Smart and big hearted and handsome as a mountain range and I tell him exactly that, I tell him this is fine because he is who he is and I am who I am, I would have nothing different from the way things are, right here, right now in this present perfect moment.

Before knowing Larry I would have wanted more. If I'd understood what I'd been given, it would have been only dimly, and I would never have found the courage to speak aloud my happiness in the moment. Now I try to pay more attention—I am a good student, if a little slow, and Larry was, after all, a teacher. These days I take care to give voice to my good fortune.

Today is a blindingly clear winter day in San Francisco. I climb to the hill above my apartment, from which it's almost possible to believe I might count the blades of grass on Mount Tamalpais, some ten miles distant. The low-slanting winter light reflects from the pastel houses of the city with such purity and directness that one would think this image would be burned into memory. And yet I could return to my apartment and in five minutes forget the salmon pink of the tower on the old Sears building on César Chavez Street, or the thin line of gilt that gleams from the steeple of St. James on Guerrero. Whereas the violets in the gardens of the French hotel where Larry and I spent our last night together— delicate lavender, lustrous from the damp of an evening thunder-shower—these I can evoke as clearly as if I were walking now a path that is years distant, while upstairs in his balconied room

Larry lies dying. What is more to the point is the way those violets evoke themselves, planting themselves in memory and denying the possibility of forgetting.

I am in France, driving Larry south and west from Tours, along the banks of the Loire. Two days later he will be dead, impossible to believe then or now, but in this moment we are driving, we are fleeing south and west, to Nantes, the Atlantic, the Gironde, the Pyrenees, Spain, Morocco, we will run as far as we can, as far as it takes. The Loire flows on our left, a broad, silvered ribbon reflecting the towering pastels of this Fragonard sky. On our right yellowing poplars shiver behind limestone-walled villages and ornate châteaux.

I drive until I am blinded by tears—Larry is so quiet, so ill. Under the crenellated medieval towers of Langeais I stop the car and turn to him. "Are you in pain?"

"No."

"We could turn back."

He presses his finger to my lips. "I'm happy being quiet here with you."

This is what I am trying to learn, the lesson Larry was teaching: the sufficiency and necessity of being quiet here with you.

But we have no choice but to cross that river, to turn and head back. Life takes the shape of an hourglass: focusing down, past and future falling away until there is nothing but this moment, this present place, the two of us amid this ancient, pastoral, autumnal countryside. Surely this is as close as I will get—surely it is as close as anyone could bear—to love pure as sunlight; to our reason for being alive.

And the sun sinks lower in the sky, the light fails, time is running out; a day, a life is racing to its end. The sunlight slants across the reed-choked Indre, shining white on the raked and graveled paths of Azay-le-Rideau, this fantasy castle. A swan sinks on extended wings, his double rising to meet him from the depths of the lake's emerald mirror. He lands, and the château's slate-sheathed towers shatter, ripple, then reassemble their inverted perfection. Stark, sharp shadows of osiers, black rapiers against green water, Larry and I set out to walk the symmetrical paths except that he cannot lift his swollen feet, shoes scrape gravel and so he turns back to the car. I turn to follow, then crouch to take up a handful of pebbles, to lodge in memory the feel of this place that I will surely never touch again in the presence of this man, this friend of my youth. The rough and raked stoniness grates against my palms, the gravel runs through my fingers but it is the thin, serpentine-flecked dirt of San Francisco, and I am standing on the hill above the apartment where I now live, where I have lived alone since Larry died. The bright white bowl of the city spreads out below. To the north the copper-red towers of the Golden Gate Bridge rise against the tawny Marin headlands.

I am in California, not in France. It is years later, I am here and he is not but love goes on, this is the lesson that I have taken, for a comfort that must and will suffice. In grief there is renewal, of love and so of life.

TEXT PERMISSIONS

The author gratefully acknowledges permission from the following sources to reprint material in their control:

Beacon Press for lines from "Poppies" from *New and Selected Poems* by Mary Oliver, copyright © 1992 by Mary Oliver.

Viking Penguin, a division of Penguin Books USA Inc. for an excerpt from "In the Ravine" by Anton Chekhov, from *The Portable Chekhov,* edited by Avrahm Yarmolinsky, (copyright) 1947, © 1968 by Viking Penguin, Inc., renewed © 1975 by Avrahm Yarmolinsky.

Alfred A. Knopf, Inc. for excerpts from *Love in the Time of Cholera* by Gabriel García Márquez, translated by Edith Grossman, copyright © 1988 by Alfred A. Knopf, Inc.

Princeton University Press for lines from *The Collected Papers of Albert Einstein,* edited by John Stachel, copyright © 1987 by Princeton University Press.

From *The Odyssey* by Homer, trans. R. Fitzgerald, copyright © 1961, 1963 by Robert Fitzgerald and renewed 1989 by Benedict RC Fitzgerald. Reprinted by permission of Vintage Books, a Division of Random House Inc.

I gratefully acknowledge the use of excerpts from the following works:

Sir Gawain and the Green Knight, (translated by Brian Stone; Penguin, 1974).

Shosha, Isaac Bashevis Singer (Farrar, Straus and Giroux, Inc., 1978).

p. 55
56 - Brother Fintan

73   ability to love

76 - cost of cutting love from the heart

92 - greatest fear: dying   love as a victory

109 - "becoming one

123 - define adulthood

143 - we fall in love for reasons

108 - hope + action

221 - desire - that short triumph
                    over fate

229 - grief / love

234 - his mother's acceptance

145 -   'what we need to know in order
          to live'

180 -   I loved even his illness and
          his dying.

210 - re-creating a family in SF

218 - his most cherished illusion - that
          I'm in control

37 He went for broke. I held out

55 - a gay teenager